ولَقَدْ يَسَّرْنَا الْقُرْءَانَ لِلذِّكْرِ فَهَلْ مِن مُّدَّكِرٍ ﴿٣٣﴾

And indeed We have made the Qur'an easy to understand and remember, then is there any that will remember? (54:32).

جديد

يسرنا القرآن

تاليف

شبير احمد بهليم

LIBRARY OF ISLAM
P.O. Box 1923
Des Plaines, IL 60017 (U.S.A)

Library of Congress Cataloging in Publication Data
Shabbir A. Behlim

Quran Made Easy
1. Islam Juvenile Literature 2. Quran
I. Title II. Islam for Children
297   BP161.2

ISBN 10: 0-933511-01-9
ISBN 13: 978-0-933511-01-9

This Revised Edition made possible
through a generous donation from

Hanif Sons, Ltd.
Lahore, Pakistan

Publisher:
Library of Islam

Distributed by:
Kazi Publications, Inc. (USA)
3023 West Belmont Avenue
Chicago IL 60618
(T) 773-267-7001; (F) 773-267-7002
email: info@kazi.org   website: www.kazi.org

FOREWORD

In the Name of Allah, the Most Beneficent, the Most Merciful

Read! In the Name of your Lord, Who has created (all that exists). He created
man from a clot. Read! And your Lord is the Most Generous, Who has taught
(the writing) by the pen, has taught man that which he knew not.   (96:1-5).

There has been a tremendous demand for a comprehensive Yassar-nal-Qur'an for the Muslim
children born in the West. Qari Hafiz Shabbir Ahmad Behlim has compiled this version basing it
on his lifelong experience of teaching the young children to read and memorize the Holy Qur'an.
We hope the Muslim community in the West will benefit from it, Insha Allah.

All the instructions have been translated into English for the benefit of English speaking learners
and teachers including the parents who are not familiar with Urdu or Arabic as a teaching medium.
This popular edition of Yassar-nal-Qur'an is complete in all respects. All the phonetic rules and
regulations of Qur'anic Arabic have been given including the Qur'anic signs for pausing, stopping
or continuing. After studying this Yassar-nal-Qur'an, a child need not go through lesson by lesson
instructions to read the Holy Qur'an. A young child should easily be able to read the Holy Qur'an
and complete it in the shortest possible time .

May Allah help all those who are eager and willing to teach and learn the Holy Qur'an through it
and may Allah bless all those who have contributed, directly or indirectly, in its completion for
the sole purpose of propagating the Message of Allah through His last Prophet, Muhammad ﷺ .

Last but not least, may Allah guide all Muslims, including our future generation, into reading,
understanding and acting upon the Holy Qur'an enabling them to draw full benefit from its wis-
dom. As Islam is a complete way of life, the knowledge of both Qur'an and Hadith is essential
to lead a happy, prosperous and meaningful life in this world, the fruit of which can be reaped
in the Hereafter, if Allah is happy with our deeds and accepts them.

Acknowledgement is due to Anjuman-e-Himayat-e-Islam, Lahore (Pakistan) for allowing us to
use their original Yassarnal Qur'an as a guideline for this adaptation. May Allah reward them,

Amin.

M.A.Qazi
Mount Prospect, IL 60056

(25) CHAPTER. Teaching the Qur'ān to the children.

554. Narrated Sa'īd bid Jubair: Those Sūras which you people call the Mufaṣṣal, (1) are the Muhkam. (2) And Ibn 'Abbās said, "Allāh's Messenger ﷺ died when I was a boy of ten years, and I had learnt the Muhkam (of the Qur'ān).

Sahih Al-Bukhari, Vol. 6, Hadith No. 554.

باب تَعْلِيمِ الصِّبْيَانِ القُرآنَ .

٥٥٤ ـ حَدَّثَتِنِى مُوسَى بنُ إسْماعِيلَ : حَدَّثَنا أَبُو عَوَانَةَ ، عَنْ أَبِى بِشْرٍ ، عَنْ سَعِيدِ بنِ جُبَيْرٍ قالَ : إنَّ الذى تَدْعُونَهُ المُفَصَّلُ هُوَ المُحْكَمُ ، قالَ : وَقالَ ابنُ عَبَّاسٍ : تُوُفِّى رَسُولُ اللهِ صلى الله عليه وسلم وأنا ابنُ عَشْرِ سِنِينَ وَقَدْ قَرأتُ المُحْكَمَ .

---

(21) CHAPTER. "The best among you (Muslims) are those who learn the Qur'ān and teach it."

545. Narrated 'Uthmān ﵁ : The Prophet ﷺ said, "The best among you (Muslims) are those who learn the Qur'ān and teach it."

Sahih Al-Bukhari, Vol. 6, Hadith No. 545.

باب خَيْرُكُمْ مَنْ تَعَلَّمَ القُرآنَ وَعَلَّمَهُ .

٥٤٥ ـ حَدَّثَنا حَجّاجُ بنُ مِنْهالٍ : حَدَّثَنا شُعْبَةُ قالَ : أخْبَرَنِى عَلْقَمَةُ بنُ مَرْثَدٍ : سَمِعْتُ سَعْدَ ابنَ عُبَيْدَةَ ، عَنْ أَبِى عَبْدِ الرَّحْمَنِ السُّلَمِى ، عَنْ عُثْمانَ رَضِىَ اللهُ عَنْهُ ، عَنِ النَّبِىِّ صلى الله عليه وسلم قالَ : خَيْرُكُمْ مَنْ تَعَلَّمَ القُرآنَ وَعَلَّمَهُ . قالَ : وأقْرأ أَبُو عَبْدِ الرَّحْمَنِ فِى إمْرَةِ عُثْمانَ حتَّى كانَ الحَجّاجُ ، قالَ : وَذَاكَ الَّذِى أقْعَدَنِى مَقْعَدِى هَذَا .

---

(1) The Muhkam are those Sūras which contain no abrogated decrees or orders.
(2) The Mufaṣṣal are the Sūras which start with Sūrat-al-Ḥujurāt to the end of the Qur'ān.

LESSON : 1

درس : ١

Jeem (j)	Thaa (th)	Taa (t)	Baa (b)	Alif (a)
ج	ث	ت	ب	ا
Raa (r)	**Zaal (z)**	**Daal (d)**	**Khaa (kh)**	**Haa (h)**
ر	ذ	د	خ	ح
Daad (d)	**Saad (s)**	**Sheen (sh)**	**Seen (s)**	**Zaa (z)**
ض	ص	ش	س	ز
Faa (f)	**Ghayn (gy)**	**Ayn (a)**	**Zaa (z)**	**Taa (t)**
ف	غ	ع	ظ	ط
Noon (n)	**Meem (m)**	**Laam (l)**	**Kaaf (k)**	**Qaaf (q)**
ن	م	ل	ك	ق
Yaa (y)	**Hamza (a)**	**Laa (la)**	**Haa (h)**	**Wau (w)**
ى	ء	لا	ه	و

LESSON : 2

مخلوط مشق

MIXED EXERCISE

درس ۲:

ا ب ب ب ب ا ب ا

ث ث ث ب ب ت ب ت

خ ح ج ث ت ث ب ج ت

ح ذ د ح ذ ذ د خ ح

س ز ر ز ز ر ز د خ

س ز ض س ض س ض ص ش

ظ ط ط ظ ط ض ص ر ش

ط غ غ ع غ ع ظ ط ض

ف ك ك ف ق ف غ ع ظ

م ل م م ل ك ق ف

و ه ه و ن ل ن ن

ي و ء ه لا لا ه لا ه

ي ى ء و ى ء ى ن

LESSON : 3

This exercise should be learned by heart by child

درس: ۳

اب یہ تختی بچے کو منہ زبانی یاد کروانی چاہیے

ا ب ت ث ج ح خ د ذ ر ز س

ش ص ض ط ظ ع غ ف ق ك

ك ل م م ن و ہ ھ لا ء ی

LESSON : 4

درس: ۴

یہ تختی مخلوط حروف کی لکھی گئی ہے تاکہ بچہ ہر ایک کو اچھی طرح شناخت کر سکے۔

This is a written exercise of mixed letters so that the child can identify each letter.

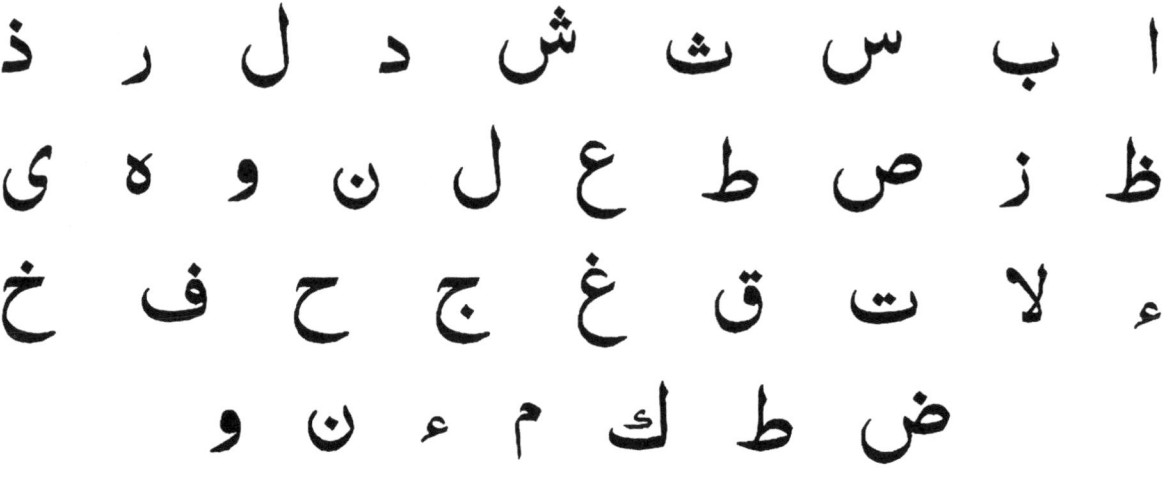

ا ب س س ش ش د ل ر ذ

ظ ز ص ط ع ل ن و ہ ی

ء لا ت ق غ ج ح ف خ

ض ط ك م ء ن و

LESSON : 5

Exercise of mixed letters

درس: ۵

مخلوط حروف کی تختی

ا ث ت ا ب ح خ د

ج ذ د ط ظ ع ش

ض ك ل ف غ ر ز ة م ء ا ى ب س

ظ غ و ه م ا لا ن لا ى خ ا ف ے ث

درس ٦: LESSON : 6

ب غ ط س ص د ف ل م ث ح خ ذ ض

ظ ع ق ن و ء ى ت ج ك ش ا ر ه ے

درس ٧: LESSON : 7

مفصلۂ ذیل حروف بھی پچھلے حروف کی طرح ایک ایک حرف جدا جدا بچے کو بتائے جائیں۔

اس جگہ حرفوں کی صرف پیوند دکھائے گئے ہیں تاکہ بچہ حروفِ تہجی کی ہر ایک شکل پہچان سکے اور قرآن مجید پڑھنے میں قطعًا دقت نہ ہو۔

تلفظ اسی طرح ہر ایک حرف کا جدا جدا بتایا جائے مثلاً بے، الف ۔ با

The following letters, like previous letters, should be taught separately (one by one). Here only the connection of letters have been shown so that the child can recognize shape of each Alphabet and there should be no difficulty in reading the Holy Qur'an.

NOTE: Similarly the pronounciation of each letter should be taught separately e.g. Ba, Alif - Ba.

ثا	ثا	ثا	تا	تا	تا	با	با	ب
خا	خا	خا	حا	حا	حا	جا	جا	ج
شا	شا	شا	سا	سا	سا	زا	را	ذا	دا

LESSON : 8	درس ۸:

Exercise of Compound Words.

پیوند والے حروف کی مشق

ظا ظا ظا طا طا طا صا صا صا

فا فا ف بغ غا غا غا بع عا عا ءا اع

كا كا كا قة قا قا قا بف بف بفذ بف

نا ذا انا ان ما ما مرا ام لا لا لا لا

یا یا ای ی ـ ء به هـ ه ها ها ها لن وا

درس ۹:
LESSON : 9

These letters should be taught separately.

یہ حروف جداجدا بتائے جائیں

تع تر تق تر تف تب تظ تد تس تس س ت

ثد ثد ثخ ثج ثج تج ثث ثش ثب ثم ث تم تغ

به نه ثو تو ثی تی ثہ تہ تر تر تر ثز ثر

ثع ثع ثط ثل ثض

6

درس :۱۰   LESSON : 10

ہر لفظ جداجدابتایاجائے۔

Each letter should be taught separately.

جش ث ش ج جت ت جب ب ج

جح جخ جج جج جش جت جب ج

جط جش جف جع جص جس جر جل جد

جی جل جن جو جم جط جق

درس :۱۱   LESSON : 11

اس مخلوط مشق کا ہر ایک حرف جداجدابتایاجائے۔

Each letter of this mixed exercise should be taught separately.

سش ش ث ست ست ت س سب ب س

شر شد سخ سج ست ست سب ست س

شو سن شم سک سف سق سع سص

سد سز سڈ سر سڈ سم سی سہ سل

سظ سس سغ سط

LESSON : 12　　　　　درس : ۱۲

Each letter to be learnt separately.　　　ہر ایک حرف الگ الگ بتائیں۔

ص ب صب ص ت صت

ص صب صت صت صت صث صج صخ صا صر

صس صص صع صع ضط ضع صف صق ضل ضم

صن ضھ صز ضس صی صک صک صو

LESSON : 13　　　　　درس : ۱۳

Learn as in previous exercises.　　　سابقہ مشقوں کی طرح پڑھیں۔

ط ب طب طت طث

ط طب طث طح طخ طا طر طر طا

طط طض طس طع طف ظق ظک ظل

ظم ظن طی طہ طل ظو طی

LESSON : 14
درس ١٤:

Ask the child to identify

بچے سے شناخت کرائیں۔

عت ت ع عب ب ع

غر عر غ‍ا غج ع غش عت غب ع

عد عغ غف غظ ع‍ع عص عس عط

غم عن ع‍ه غش غل عک عک عق

عی غ‍ه عو عض غم غظ عخ

LESSON : 15
درس ١٥:

To be learnt separately.

ہر ایک حرف جدا جدا بتایا جائے۔

فت ت ف فب ب ف

ف‍ا فر ق‍ا فخ فخ فج فت فب ف

قع فع قض فش فس فض فظ قط فز فر

فی فو فن ف‍ه قم قم فک فک قق فف

9

LESSON : 16   درس : ١٦

Put finger on each letter and ask the child to identify it.   ہر ایک حرف پر انگلی رکھ کر بچے سے شناخت کرائیں۔

ک ب کب کت کش

ک کب کت کش کت کج کع کح کد کذ کر کڈ

کر کز کع کغ کک ککـ کل کہ کی کق کن

ل لش لج لع لغ لڈ لذ لر لڑ لز لل لق

لو لہ لی کن لک لمـ کمـ لی

LESSON : 17   درس : ١٧

Each letter to be learnt separately.   جدا جدا حرف پڑھائیں۔

م مب مط مڈ مڈ مڈ مز مز مڈ می مخ

ن ذ نب نت نر نو نی نف نف نف نع نص نق

نف فق فق نف نن نو فو نل نس نمـ نر

فل نمـ فمـ نہ مہ فو نو مو نی فی ق

LESSON : 18	درس : ۱۸

Each letter to be learnt separately.

بچے سے ایک ایک حرف کا نام پوچھا جائے۔

ہ ب ھب ھ ۂ ت ھت

ھ ھب ھت ھث ھج ھج ھج ھد ھد ھر

ھر ھز ھس ھش ھص ھض ھط ھظ

ھع ھف ھق ھك ھک ھم ھم ھن ھ

ھو ھی ھه ھة ھة

LESSON : 19	درس : ۱۹

Each letter to be learnt separately.

ہر ایک حرف جدا جدا بتایا جائے

ی ب یب یی ت یت

ی یب یت یث یج یج یث ید یر یر یر

یز یس یش یض یص یط یظ یع یغ

یف یق یك یک یل یم یم ین یو یہ

یٰ تی تق یق یو تو تہ یی یم تن تو

سہ حَرفی تختی

THREE LETTERED EXERCISE

مندرجہ ذیل حروف کو بھی پچھلے اسباق کی طرح جداجدا بچے کے ذہن نشین کرائیے

THE FOLLOWING LETTERS SHOULD ALSO BE UNDERSTOOD BY THE CHILD SEPARATELY AS BEFORE.

LESSON : 20   Child to identify.   بچے پیچانے   درس ۲۰:

ث   ت   ت   ب   ا

بات   حدث   اثم   ثفر   بثت   ثبت   ابد

امن   رفث   ثلث   ترك   ثمن   مات   تبت

بتث   کتب   کبر   بسط   برز   بدر

LESSON : 21   درس ۲۱:

Ask the child to identify as before.   سابقہ طریق سے بچے سے شناخت کرائی جائے۔

خ   ح   ج

جلد   یلج   نجح   حجب   جلب   جبل   جمل

خطف   حبط   خبر   اخذ

LESSON : 22	درس : ۲۲

ہر ایک حرف پر انگلی رکھ کر بچے سے شناخت کرائیں ۔ اور ہر ایک حرف جدا جدا بتایا جائے ۔

Put finger on each letter and ask the child to identify it. Each letter to be taught separately.

ر   ذ   د

دخل خدع رقد ردف قدم مرض ابر

رمض رحم کرم غرب دفع امر دمر

اذن ریب ذلك ذلل رمز رجع صلد

ولد   ونہز   خذار

LESSON : 23	درس : ۲۳

بچے سے شناخت کرائی جائے ۔

Ask the child to identify.

ز   س   ش

زمر شرر سرر سمع شفع سنخ سلد

شرف سفر شجر زہد زور خور شاد

رزق ازں حزں شکر سرف سفہ

شجر حسن سلم عزم

13

LESSON : 24
Ask the child to recognize
each letter separately.

درس : ۲٤

ہر ایک حرف بچے سے الگ الگ بُو چھا جائے۔

ص   ض   ط   ظ

صبر   ضرر   شطط   صنع   صرف   ضلت

ضلل   غاظ   ظهر   طمس   طلق   بطش

ضحك   قطع   سخط   حضر   ارض   وصل

وضم   قضی   غضب   ظلم

LESSON : 25

درس : ۲۵

ہر ایک حرف کی شکل پر انگلی رکھ کر بچے کو بتایا جائے کہ یہ فلاں حرف ہے۔ پھر اس سے ان حروف کی شناخت کرائی جائے تاکہ بچہ ہر ایک حرف کو مختلف شکلیں و پیوند سے اچھی طرح واقف ہو جائے۔

Put finger on each letter and guide the child in learning each letter. Then he should be asked to identify the same so that he becomes conversant with each shape and joint of various letters.

ع   غ   ف

غفر   علم   غضب   فقر   عظم   فضح

فصح   غلب   فجر   عشا   غرب   غفل   فسع

عمل   عفی   خسف   عشر   عین   فسد   عجب

LESSON : 26

درس :٢٦

Child should identify by himself.

بچہ خود شناخت کرے۔

ل   ك   ق

قمر   كمل   كرہ   كفل   قدر   رزق   قطر

قصر   لمح   برق   مزق   لذب   نجل   لعل

قسم   قشر   كفر   طلع   الہ   قهر

LESSON : 27

درس :٢٧

Put finger on each letter and tell the child to name it.

حرف پہ انگلی رکھ کر بچے سے حرف کا نام پوچھیں۔

و   ن   م

نصر   ملك   يوم   دين   نهب   نزل   نصت

ذلك   علم   بمن   وهم   ولو   مثل   نعل

نعم   وسع   ختم   نفس   طور   نفع   طمع

حسن   وهن

15

LESSON : 28

درس ۲۸:

Keep on asking the child to identify each letter, and learn each letter separately.

بچے سے شناخت بھی کراتے جائیے اور تمام حروف الگ الگ بتاتے جائیں۔

ہ   ء   ی

عنب   هزو   هدای   جئت   یلج   یوم   های

همس   یعظ   قیل   شیء   هوی   خیر   یلد

معه   یؤمن   حیث   منی   رهن   همن

همه   حیت   نیل   هلع   یعه   یلر   عمی

پیوستہ حُرُوف
LINKED LETTERS

LESSON : 29

درس ۲۹:

Compound words should be identified by the child. Put your finger on each letter and gently ask the child what letter is it?

پیوستہ حروف کی شناخت بچے سے کرائی جائے۔ ہر ایک حرف پر انگلی رکھ کر بچے سے نہایت پیار کے ساتھ دریافت کیا جائے کہ یہ حرف کونسا ہے؟

فاستغفر   مستقیم   نستعین   انعمت

کذلك   لمیمسسنی   بشر   محسنین

سنين   يضع   دخلوا   اذا   ان الملوك

نعت   والسماء   على الملٰئكة   والذين

LESSON : 30   درس : ۳۰

اگر چہ حروف الفاظ کی صورت میں بامعنی ہو گئے ہیں مگر یہاں بھی بچے کو صرف حروف ہی کی شناخت کرائی جائے تاکہ بچہ ہر ایک حرف کے پیوند و جوڑ کو اچھی طرح سمجھ جائے۔

Although letters in the shape of words have meanings, but here also the child should be asked to identify each letter separately so that he may become familiar with their shapes and the way they are connected to each other.

بالصلوة   رحمتنا   مخلصا   جعلنا

من الجنة   للناس   لخرجنا   بالكتب

مضغة   خلقنكم   يستبشرون   يظلمون

صفصفا   قاعا   طغى الشيطن   لا تعلمون

بمستيقنين   فى السمٰوت   لا يبلى   لعلهم

فما   انفسكم   لٰكنكم   فقست   يستعتبون

الجحيم   المصّيطرون

اعراب یعنی زبر زیر پیش

VOWEL POINTS

I.E. FATHA (ZABAR), KASRA (ZER), DAMMA (PESH)

بچے کو زبر، زیر، پیش کی اچھی طرح سے شناخت کرائی جائے۔ زبر زیر کا فرق صرف اوپر نیچے واقع ہونے کے سبب بچے کو سمجھایا جائے۔

مگر پیش کی شکل اور اس کا حرف اوپر ہی واقع ہونا بچے کے ذہن نشین کرایا جائے اور مندرجہ ذیل شکل سے زبر، زیر اور پیش بچے کو بخوبی سمجھا دیے جائیں۔

۱ شکل ۱ زبر کو ظاہر کرتی ہے۔

۲ شکل ۲ پیش کو ظاہر کرتی ہے۔

۳ شکل ۳ زیر کو ظاہر کرتی ہے۔

The child should identify Fatha (Zabar), Kasra (Zer), Damma (Pesh) well. The difference between Fatha (Zabar) and Kasra (Zer), being above and below, should be taught. He should be made to understand that Damma (Pesh) is always above the letter. With the help of the following sketch, the child should understand Fatha (Zabar), Kasra (Zer) and Damma (Pesh) very well.

Figure I shows Fatha (Zabar), Figure 2 shows Kasra (Zer), Figure 3 shows Damma (Pesh).

LESSON : 31   درس ۳۱:

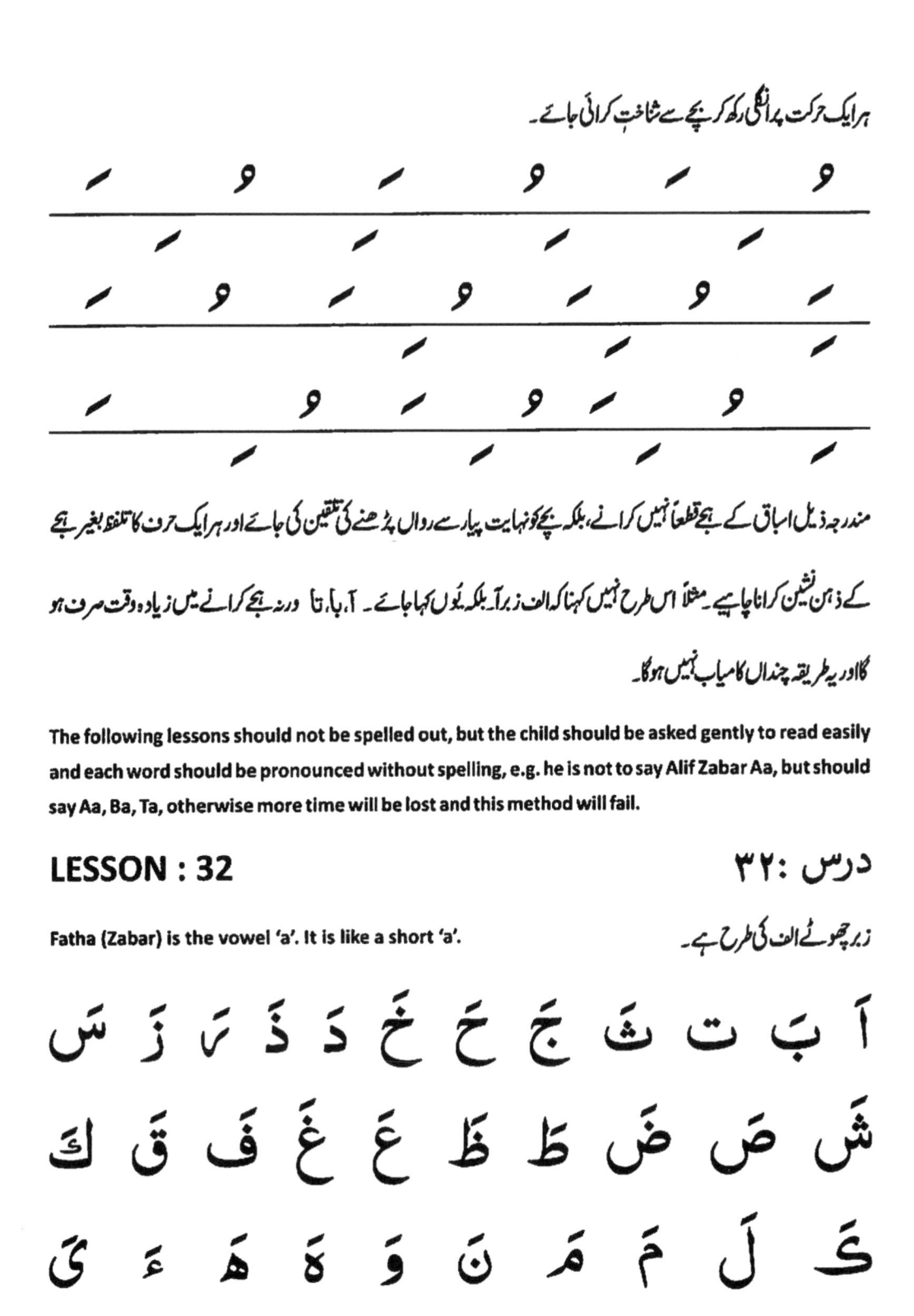

ہر ایک حرکت پر انگلی رکھ کر بچے سے شناخت کرائی جائے۔

مندرجہ ذیل اسباق کے ہجے قطعاً نہیں کرانے، بلکہ بچے کو نہایت پیار سے رواں پڑھنے کی تلقین کی جائے اور ہر ایک حرف کا تلفظ بغیر ہجے کے ذہن نشین کرانا چاہیے۔ مثلاً اس طرح نہیں کہنا کہ الف زبر آ بلکہ یوں کہا جائے ۔ آ، با، تا۔ ورنہ بچے کرانے میں زیادہ وقت صرف ہو گا اور یہ طریقہ چنداں کامیاب نہیں ہوگا۔

The following lessons should not be spelled out, but the child should be asked gently to read easily and each word should be pronounced without spelling, e.g. he is not to say Alif Zabar Aa, but should say Aa, Ba, Ta, otherwise more time will be lost and this method will fail.

LESSON : 32

درس : ۳۲

Fatha (Zabar) is the vowel 'a'. It is like a short 'a'.

زبر چھوٹے الف کی طرح ہے۔

أَ بَ تَ ثَ جَ حَ خَ دَ ذَ رَ زَ سَ

شَ صَ ضَ طَ ظَ عَ غَ فَ قَ كَ

كَ لَ مَ نَ وَ هَ ءَ یَ

LESSON : 33

The child should name the following letters.

درس : ۳۳

بچہ مندرجہ ذیل حروف کے نام بتائے۔

ا ب ت ج د س ط ف

اَ بَ طَ عَ غَ دَ وَ ھَ صَ شَ مَ

ضَ قَ ھَ كَ ظَ خَ زَ طَ ئَ فَ نَ

LESSON : 34

The following compound letters should be taught as above but together.

درس : ۳۴

نیچے لکھے ہوئے مرکب حروف کا تلفظ اوپر کی مشق کے مطابق بتایا جائے لیکن اکٹھا۔

بَدَ مَدَ فَدَ قَدَ جَدَ اَبَ قَبَ كَبَ

زَرَ جَرَ مَنَ فَقَ ذَقَ تَبَ ثَبَ بَتَ

جَبَ دَرَ حَرَ قَلَ نَلَ زَلَ نَمَ قُمَّ

LESSON : 35

Both letters should be pronounced together

درس : ۳۵

دونوں حرفوں کا تلفظ اکٹھا کرانا چاہیے۔

طَف فَق عَف غَظ فَت فَز مَل نَدَ

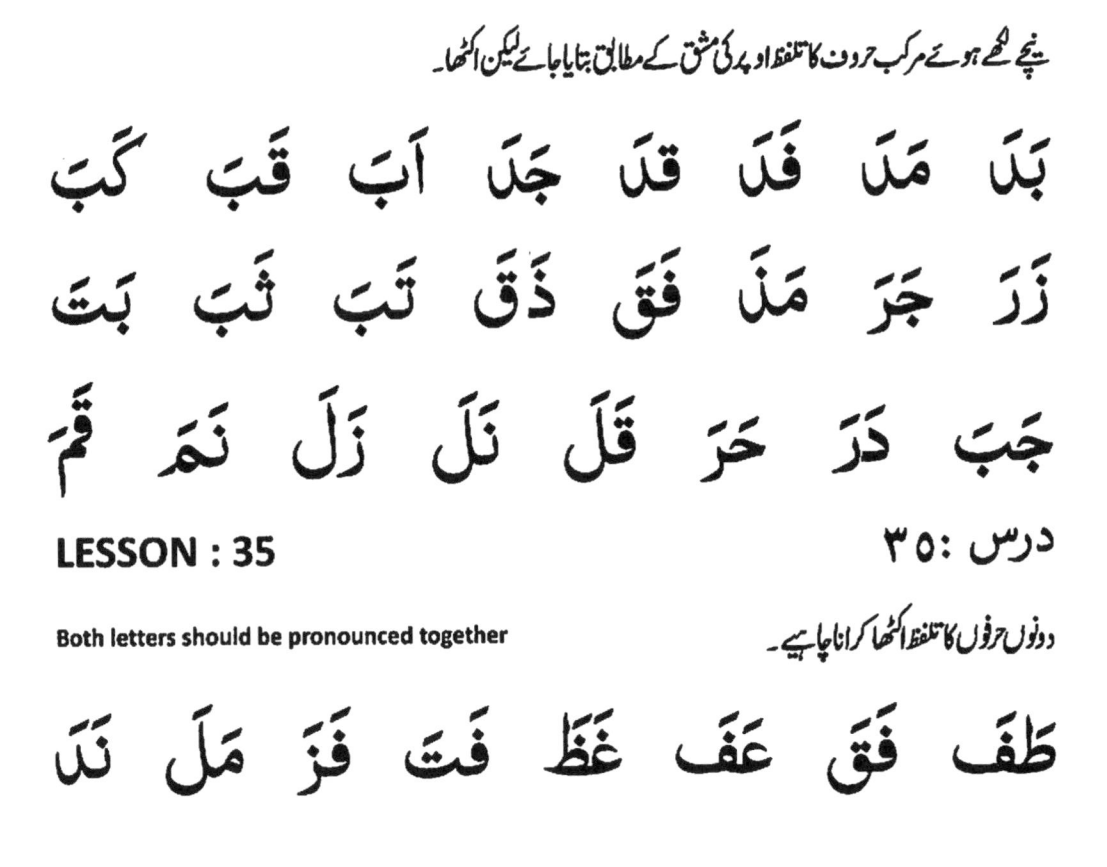

20

خَفَ جَفَ طَغَ طَغَ عَشَ طَشَ عَسَ صَدَ

صَفَ بَدَ وَفَ سَفَ شَقَ رَفَ فَدَ

LESSON : 36

درس ٣٦:

Pronunciation should be taught as in previous exercises but together.

سابقہ مشقوں کی طرح تلفظ بتایا جائے مگر اکٹھا۔

زَرَ مَنَ جَزَ کَنَ لَنَ مَتَ فَتَ صَرَ

بَرَ دَب نَب زَدَ نَدَ بَتَ اَتَ حَرَ

تَرَ گَلَ دَمَ جَرَ دَرَ ضَرَ شَب حَج

LESSON : 37

درس ٣٧:

Kasra (Zer) is the vowel 'e'. It is like a short 'e'.

زیر چھوٹی یا کی طرح ہے۔

اِ بِ تِ ثِ جِ حِ خِ دِ ذِ رِ زِ سِ

شِ صِ ضِ طِ ظِ عِ غِ فِ قِ كِ

کِ لِ مِ نِ وِ هِ ءِ یِ

LESSON : 38

درس ۳۸:

چونکہ پچھلے اسباق میں بچے زبر والے یعنی مفتوح حروف کو اچھی طرح سے ذہن نشین کر چکا ہے۔ یہاں زیر والے یعنی مکسور حروف کی مشق لکھی جاتی ہے۔ بچہ ان حروف کے صرف نام بتائے۔

Because, in the previous lessons, the child has understood the letters with Fatha (Zabar), here an exercise with Kasra (Zer) is given. The child should only name these letters, separately.

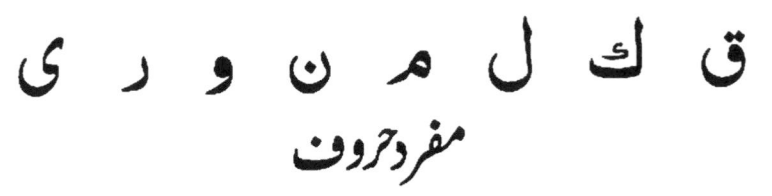

ق ك ل م ن و ر ی

مفرد حروف

SINGLE LETTERS

The child should learn pronunciation only.

بچے کو صرف تلفظ بتایا جائے۔

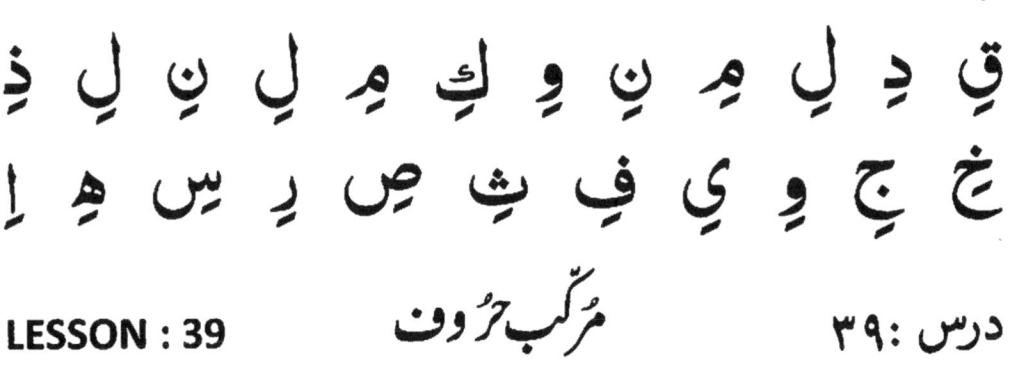

LESSON : 39

درس ۳۹:

مُرَکَّب حُرُوف

COMPOUND LETTERS

Both letters to be pronounced together

دونوں حروف کا تلفظ اکٹھا ادا کیا جائے۔

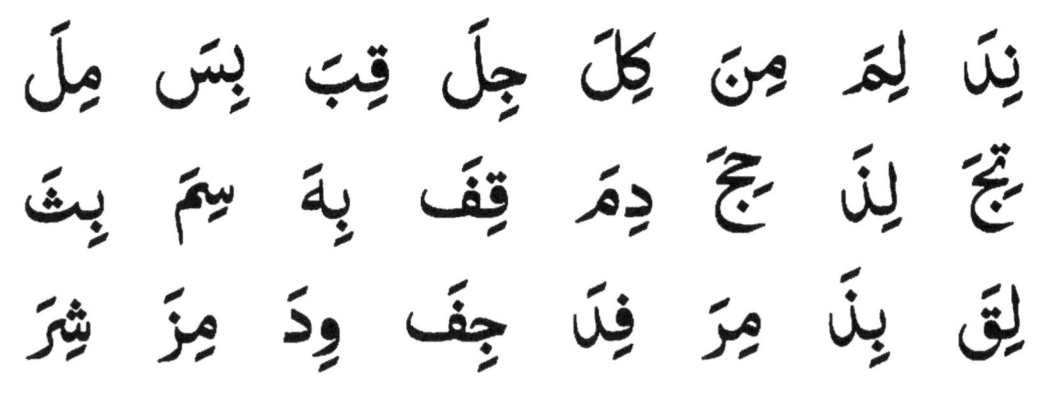

نِك اِذ حِم بِمَ فِرَ رِبَ رِخَ بِعَ

LESSON : 40

درس : ٤٠

Damma (Pesh) is the vowel 'u'. It has a sound in between 'o' and 'u'.

پیش چھوٹے واؤ کی طرح ہے

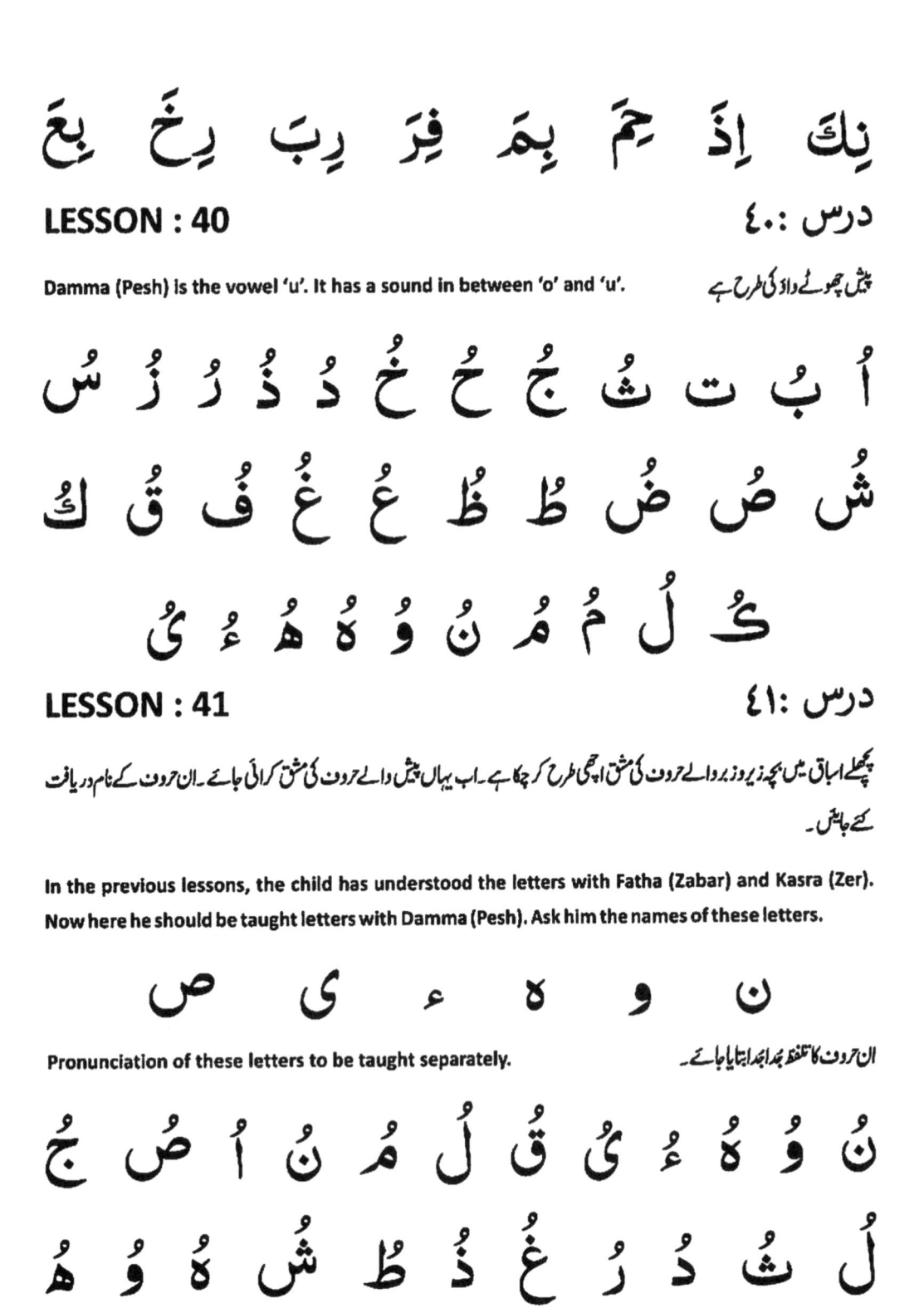

أُ بُ تُ ثُ جُ حُ خُ دُ ذُ رُ سُ

شُ صُ ضُ طُ ظُ عُ غُ فُ قُ كُ

كُ لُ مُ نُ وُ هُ ءُ ئُ

LESSON : 41

درس : ٤١

پچھلے اسباق میں بچہ زیر و زبر والے حروف کی مشق اچھی طرح کر چکا ہے۔ اب یہاں پیش والے حروف کی مشق کرائی جائے۔ ان حروف کے نام دریافت کیے جائیں۔

In the previous lessons, the child has understood the letters with Fatha (Zabar) and Kasra (Zer). Now here he should be taught letters with Damma (Pesh). Ask him the names of these letters.

ص ء ی ء ہ و ن

Pronunciation of these letters to be taught separately.

ان حروف کا تلفظ جدا جدا بتایا جائے۔

نُ وُ هُ ءُ ئُ قُ لُ مُ نُ أُ صُ جُ

لُ شُ دُ رُ غُ ذُ طُ شُ هُ وُ هُ

LESSON : 42   مُرَکّب حُرُوف   درس : ٤٢

COMPOUND LETTERS

Compound pronunciation to be taught.   اکٹھا تلفظ بتایا جائے۔

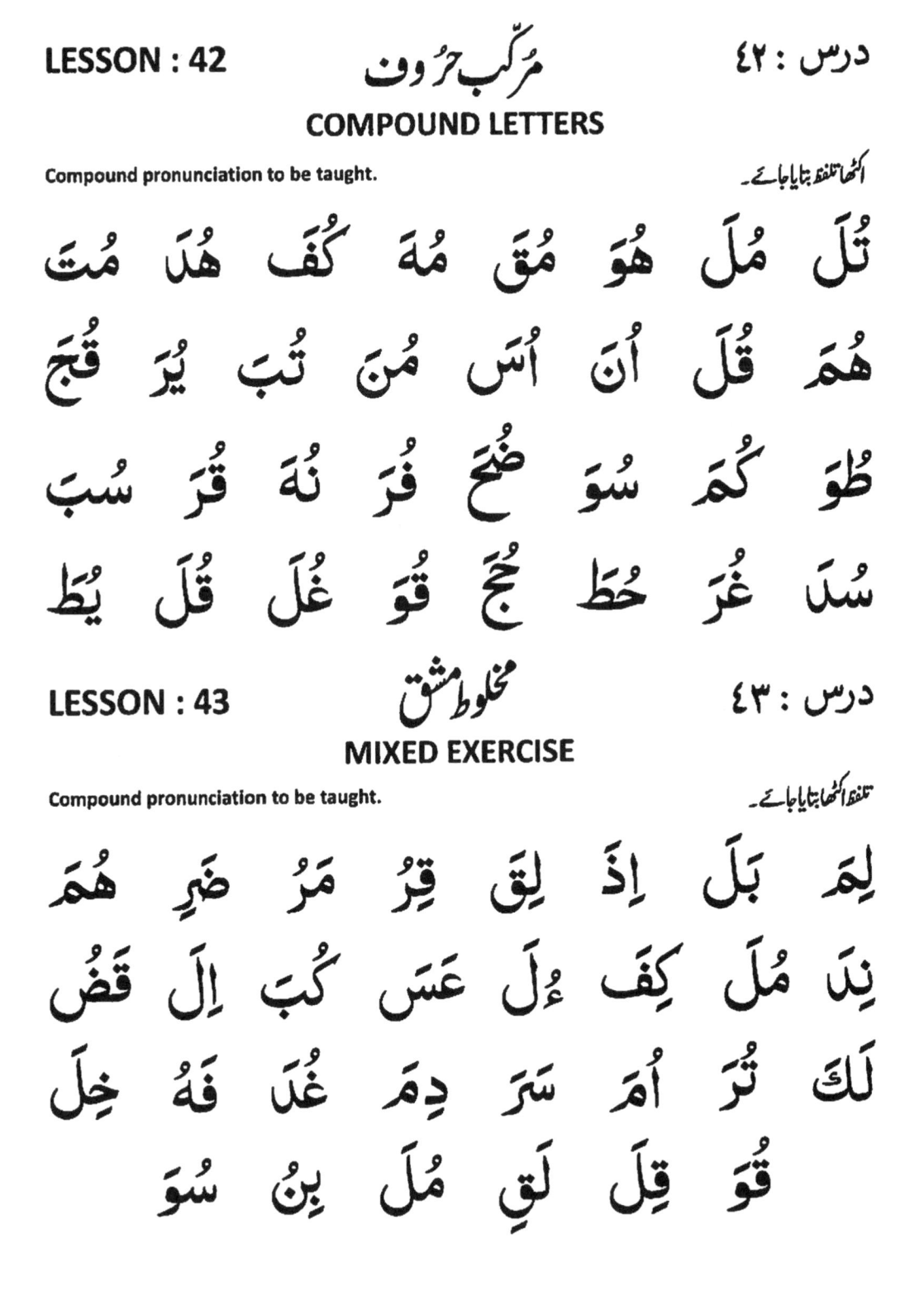

تُلَ   مُلَ   هُوَ   مُقَ   مُهَ   کُفَ   هُلَ   مُتَ

هُمَ   قُلَ   اَنَ   اُسَ   مُنَ   تُبَ   یُرَ   قُجَ

طُوَ   کُمَ   سُوَ   ضُحَ   فُرَ   نُهَ   قُرَ   سُبَ

سُدَ   غُرَ   حُطَ   حُجَ   قُوَ   غُلَ   قُلَ   یُطَ

LESSON : 43   مَخلُوط مشق   درس : ٤٣

MIXED EXERCISE

Compound pronunciation to be taught.   تلفظ اکٹھا بتایا جائے۔

لِمَ   بَلَ   اِذَ   لِقَ   قِرُ   مَرُ   ضَرِ   هُمَ

نِدَ   مُلَ   کِفَ   اُلِ   عَسَ   کُبَ   اِلَ   قَضُ

لَک   تُرَ   اُمَ   سَرَ   دِمَ   غُلَ   فَهُ   خِلَ

قُوَ   قِلَ   لَقِ   مُلَ   بِن   سُوَ

ھدایت

پچھلے اسباق میں بچہ اعراب کی پوری پوری شناخت کر چکا ہے ۔ یعنی زبر، زیر، پیش کو الگ الگ پہچان چکا ہے ۔ نیز تینوں حرکات کی مخلوط مشق بھی پڑھ چکا ہے اور یہ مشقیں بھی دوحرفی تھیں اور ان کے تلفظ میں اس امر کا زیادہ خیال رکھا گیا تھا کہ مرکب حرفوں میں کوئی ایسا تلفظ پیدا نہ ہونے پائے جو زبان پر ثقیل معلوم ہو بلکہ اس بات کی کوشش کی گئی ہے کہ مرکب حروف کے تمام الفاظ قرآن مجید کے درج کئے جائیں تا کہ آنے والے اسباق سے بچہ قبل از وقت واقف ہو جائے ۔

In the previous lessons, the child has understood the vowel marks very well, i.e. he has learnt the Fatha (Zabar), kasra (Zer), and Damma (Pesh) separately. Also he has read mixed exercises of all three vowel marks, and these were two-lettered exercises, and in the pronunciation of these letters, it was kept in mind that no pronunciation of compound letters should be heavy on the tongue, But an effort has been made that all combined letters are words from the Holy Qur'an so that child becomes already familiarized with the lessons that will follow.

LESSON : 44   درس : ٤٤

Pronunciation of three-lettered words, exercise of letters with Fatha (Zabar)

سہ حرفی تختی کا تلفظ، مفتوح حروف کی مشق ۔

مَثَلْ   حَضَرَ   نَظَرَ   شَرَفَ   بَدَرَ   نَسَكَ

قَدَرَ   عَدَلَ   نَذَرَ   حَمَلَ   قَبَلَ   تَرَكَ

نَصَرَ   عَمَلَ   كَفَرَ   صَبَرَ   كَفَلَ   بَرَقَ

LESSON : 45   درس : ٤٥

Pronunciation only be taught.

صرف تلفظ بتایا جائے ۔

شَرَكَ   عَمَلَ   اَزَرَ   غَرَقَ   نَذَرَ   خَسَفَ

$$\text{مَكَثَ} \quad \text{فَتَحَ} \quad \text{عَدَلَ} \quad \text{اَجَرَ} \quad \text{كَفَرَ} \quad \text{شَرَفَ}$$

$$\text{حَشَرَ} \quad \text{عَمَلَ} \quad \text{حَمَدَ} \quad \text{بَدَدَ} \quad \text{قَمَرَ} \quad \text{اَبَدَ}$$

LESSON : 46

درس : ٤٦

As in previous exercises, pronunciation to be taught.

سابقہ مشقوں کی طرح تلفظ بتایا جائے۔

$$\text{مَرَدَ} \quad \text{خَلَقَ} \quad \text{اَمَدَ} \quad \text{نَسَكَ} \quad \text{عَبَسَ} \quad \text{فَرَضَ}$$

$$\text{عَدَدَ} \quad \text{غَفَرَ} \quad \text{بَصَرَ} \quad \text{نَشَفَ} \quad \text{كَسَبَ} \quad \text{غَسَقَ}$$

$$\text{اَمَنَ} \quad \text{قَتَلَ} \quad \text{رَزَقَ} \quad \text{قَمَرَ} \quad \text{كَتَبَ} \quad \text{مَكَثَ}$$

LESSON : 47

درس : ٤٧

Pronunciation only to be taught.

صرف تلفظ بتایا جائے۔

$$\text{اِبِلِ} \quad \text{بَقِى} \quad \text{لَقِى} \quad \text{اَذِنَ} \quad \text{خَشِىَ} \quad \text{حَمِدَ}$$

$$\text{نَسِىَ} \quad \text{يَلِجُ} \quad \text{وَلَجَ} \quad \text{بَلَدِ} \quad \text{وَلِدَ} \quad \text{اِرَمَ}$$

$$\text{خَلَدَ} \quad \text{اَنَسَ} \quad \text{فَتَحَ} \quad \text{بَلَغَ} \quad \text{اَمَرَ} \quad \text{كَذِبَ}$$

LESSON : 48

درس : ٤٨

Pronunciation only to be taught.

صرف تلفظ بتایا جائے۔

$$\text{سَمِعَ} \quad \text{حَسِبَ} \quad \text{عَمِلَ} \quad \text{عِنَبَ} \quad \text{عَلِمَ} \quad \text{مَلِك}$$

26

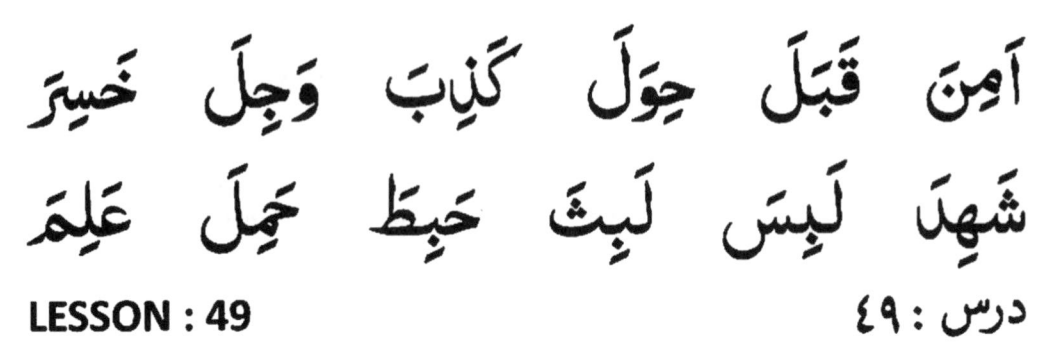

LESSON : 49   ٤٩ : درس

مرفوع حروف یعنی پیش والے حروف کی مشق

EXERCISE OF LETTERS WITH DAMMA (PESH) OVER THEM

Pronunciation only should be taught.   صرف تلفظ ہی بتایا جائے ۔

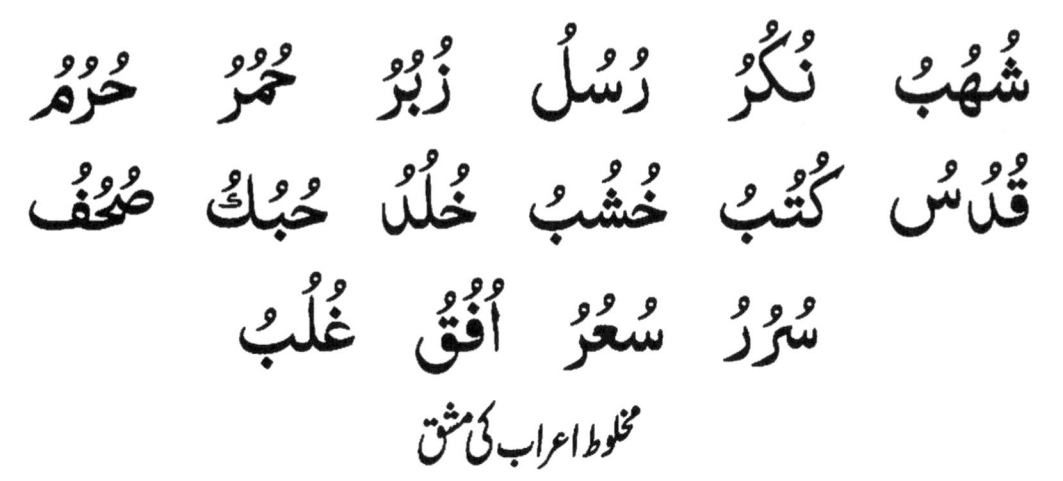

مخلوط اعراب کی مشق

EXERCISE OF MIXED VOWEL POINTS

LESSON : 50   ٥٠ : درس

Pronunciation only to be taught.   صرف تلفظ ہی بتایا جائے ۔

وَلَجَ   وَصَلَ   فَضَلَ   مَثَلَ   دَخَلَ   ذٰلِكَ

بَلَغَ   عَلِمَ   حَسِبَ   أَذِنَ   مَلِكَ   كَذِبَ

LESSON : 51

Pronunciation to be taught.

LESSON : 52

Pronunciation should be taught.

LESSON : 53

Pronunciation should be taught.

رَفَثَ   شَرُفَ   عَدَادَ   كَفَلَ   عَصِمَ

يَعِدُ   بَلَدُ   يَئِسَ   سُلِخَ   نُفِخَ

مخلوط اعراب کی مشق

LESSON : 54   **MIXED EXERCISE**   درس : ٥٤

Exercise of four-lettered words.   چار حرفے الفاظ کی مشق

فَبَعَثَ   فَشَرِبَ   وَرَفَعَ   وَذَكَرَ   دَرَجَةَ

فَسُبُلَ   وَصَدَفَ   فَشَهِدَ   فَنَسِيَ   فَاَخَذَ

فَمَثَلُ   فَخَرَجَ   فَخَلَقَ   فَلَقِيَ   فَسَجَدَ

فَمَكَرُ   وَوَضَعَ   فَفَرَعَ   فَسَفَرَ   كَمَثَلِ

فَجَعَلَ   فَسَجَدَ   فَجَدَلَ   فَشَطَرَ   وَكَفَرَ

هدایت: الف مدّہ کو اعراب والے الفاظ کے ساتھ ملا کر پڑھنے کا طریقہ۔ یہ الف صرف آواز کو بلند کرنے اور کھینچ کر پڑھنے کیلئے لکھا جاتا ہے۔ بچے کو ہجے کرانے کی کوئی ضرورت نہیں۔ صرف تلفظ بتا دیا جائے خود بخود پڑھتا چلا جائے گا۔

Method of reading Alif Madda with letters carrying vowel marks. This is used to lengthen and heighten the sound of long vowels. The child should not be asked to spell, only pronunciation should be taught. He will read easily.

LESSON : 55	درس ٥٥ :

با تا ثا جا حا خا

بَا تَا ثَا جَا حَا خَا دَا ذَا

رَا زَا سَا شَا صَا ضَا طَا ظَا

عَا غَا فَا قَا کَا لَا مَا نَا

وَا هَا ئَا یَا

LESSON : 56	درس ٥٦ :

صرف تلفظ بتایا جائے۔

Pronunciation only should be taught.

ب ن ا   ص ف ا   س ب ا

بَنَا صَفَا سَبَا عَلَا نِدَا مَلَا عَدَا عَسَا

هَوَا بَلَا بَرَا عَفَا شِفَا قِفَا اُنَا لِقَا

LESSON : 57	درس ٥٧ :

صرف تلفظ بتایا جائے۔

Pronunciation only should be taught.

مُهَا سَمَا لهٰنَا اَسَفَا اَصَدَا شَطَطَا کَذِبَا

30

بِمَا عَجِبَا عَمَلًا عَدَدًا قَالَ مَثَلًا كَانَ

جَاهَدَ حَالَ تَابَ بَابَ

LESSON : 58
درس : ۵۸

Pronunciation only should be taught.
صرف تلفظ بتایا جائے۔

عَالِمُ مَالِكِ قَامَ زَارَ كَامِلُ حَامِلُ قَادِرُ

عَاذِلُ عَادِلٌ شَاكِرُ رَازِقٌ بَاسِطٌ خَالِقٌ

كَافِرُ غَافِرُ وَاهِبُ وَاحِدُ لَازِبُ نَالَ

مَاتَ فَاتَ بَاتَ صَارَ جَارَ عَادَ

حَاقَ عَدَا بَلَا نَوَا لَهَا نِدَا

LESSON : 59
درس : ۵۹

Pronunciation only to be taught.
صرف تلفظ بتایا جائے۔

مَحَارِبُ مَغَارِبُ مَشَارِقُ مُسَافِرُ مُقَاتِلُ

مُجَاهِدُ مُوَافِقٌ مَرَافِقُ مَرَاضِعُ مَلَابِسُ

سَنَابِلُ مَسَاجِدُ مِهَادُ مَرَاحِلُ أَرَاذِلُ

LESSON : 60

درس : ٦٠

Pronunciation only should be taught.

صرف تلفظ بتایا جائے۔

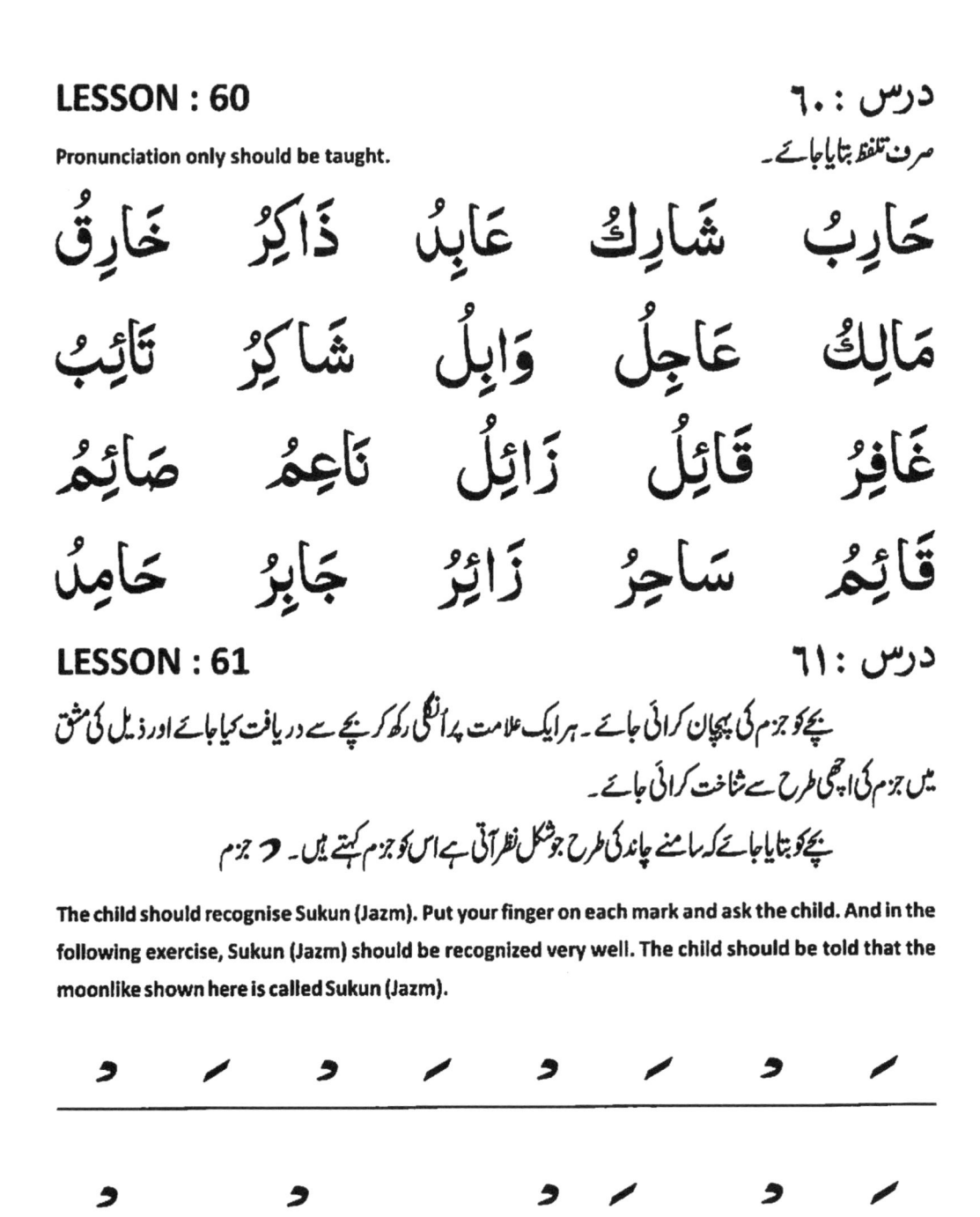

خَارِقُ   ذَاكِرُ   عَابِدُ   شَارِكُ   حَارِبُ

تَائِبُ   شَاكِرُ   وَابِلُ   عَاجِلُ   مَالِكُ

صَائِمُ   نَاعِمُ   زَائِلُ   قَائِلُ   غَافِرُ

حَامِدُ   جَابِرُ   زَائِرُ   سَاحِرُ   قَائِمُ

LESSON : 61

درس : ٦١

بچے کو جزم کی پہچان کرائی جائے۔ ہر ایک علامت پر انگلی رکھ کر بچے سے دریافت کیا جائے اور ذیل کی مشق میں جزم کی اچھی طرح سے شناخت کرائی جائے۔

بچے کو بتایا جائے کہ سامنے چاند کی طرح جو شکل نظر آتی ہے اس کو جزم کہتے ہیں۔ ﺩ جزم

The child should recognise Sukun (Jazm). Put your finger on each mark and ask the child. And in the following exercise, Sukun (Jazm) should be recognized very well. The child should be told that the moonlike shown here is called Sukun (Jazm).

LESSON : 62   درس : ٦٢

بچے کو صرف تلفظ بتایا جائے۔ بچے کرانے کی قطعاً ضرورت نہیں۔ زبر اور جزم والے حروف کا پیوند۔

Teach pronunciation only; no need to spell at all. Combination of letters with Fatha (Zabar).

لَمُ   كُمْ   هَمْ   حَدُ   قَدُ

صَفْ   مَرْ   عَمْ   لَنْ   هَمْ   حَلْ   قَدْ

فُلْ   مَنْ   اَمْ   كَفْ   خَفْ   بَرْ   بَلْ   هَبْ

حَلْ   نَلْ   مَلْ   بَلْ   جَلْ   كُلْ   هَلْ   وَلْ

ظَمْ   جَمْ   ذَمْ   ضَمْ   يَمْ   فُمْ   غَمْ   عَمْ

رَنْ   ظَنْ   عَنْ   بَنْ   اَنْ   دَنْ   فَنْ   مَنْ

LESSON : 63   درس : ٦٣

صرف تلفظ بتایا جائے۔

Pronunciation only to be taught.

جَبْ   كَمْ   دَمْ   حَبْ

طَفْ   كَفْ   صَفْ   شَلْ   جَبْ   قَتْ   اَتْ   كُمْ   حَبْ

سَبْ   اَبْ   كَلْ   غَلْ   مَلْ   فَظْ   حَظْ   قَلْ

مَنْ   اَنْ   لَمْ   كُمْ   وَدْ   تَكْ   عَمْ   دَمْ

LESSON : 64

Pronunciation only to be taught.

درس : ٦٤

صرف تلفظ بتایا جائے۔

جَمْ تَلْ حَلْ اَلْ سَلْ عَنْ نَفْ شَقْ

ذَلْ فَضْ نُجْ فَعْ صَرْ عَسْ دَعْ مَعْ

سہ حرفی تختی

THREE-LETTERED EXERCISE

LESSON : 65

Pronunciation only should be taught.

درس : ٦٥

بچے کو صرف تلفظ بتایا جائے۔

اَمْرُ فَضْلُ رَحْمٌ بَرْقٌ عَبْدُ حَمْلُ

بَحْرُ حَرْب قَبْرُ صَبْرُ حَبْلُ اَجْرُ

اَدَمَ خَتَمَ ثَمَنْ وَمَنْ اَمَنْ حَسَنْ

LESSON : 66

درس : ٦٦

Pronunciation only to be taught as in previous lessons. گزشتہ اسباق کی طرح صرف تلفظ ہی بتایا جائے۔

فَرَقَ اَرْضُ نَسْلُ رَعْدُ قَبْلَ دَخَلَ

نَجَمَ لَقَدْ كَمَنْ مَرَضْ

LESSON : 67
مخلوط مشق
MIXED EXERCISE
۶۷ : درس

اَنَسَ عَبَسَ اَهَلَ حَسَدَ نَفَسَ سَعٰی

بَطَشَ مَرْءُ عَصَرَ بَصَرَ قَرَضَ

LESSON : 68
Pronunciation only
to be taught.
چار حرفی تختی
FOUR-LETTERED EXERCISE
۶۸ : درس
صرف تلفظ بتایا جائے۔

اُدَمَ اَعْرَضَ اَسْفَلَ اَظْلَمَ اَكْرَمَ اَعْلَمُ

خَلَقَ اَرْزَقَ اَثْبَتَ اَسْلَمَ اَنْزَلَ اَنْعَمَ

LESSON : 69
مخلوط مشق
MIXED EXERCISE
۶۹ : درس

اَفْلَحَ اَصْلَحَ اَنْتَ ظَلَمْتَ اَكْبَرَ اَفْرَغَ

اَبْلَغَ اَجْعَلَ اَمْهَلَ اٰزَرَ اَلْهَمَ اَصْدَرَ

اَصْدَقَ اَغْفَرَ اَمَرَهٗ لَقَدْ اَجْمَلُ كَافِرٌ

LESSON : 70
Pronunciation only to be taught.
۷۰ : درس
صرف تلفظ بتایا جائے۔

اَرْسَلَ اَصْبَرَ اَمْلَا اَصْدَقَ اَحْسَنَ

أَعۡرَضَ   أَرۡذَلَ   أَخۡسَرَ   أَبۡلَغَ   أَمۡكَرَ

زیر اور جزم والے حروف کا ملانا

COMBINING LETTERS WITH KASRA (ZER) AND SUKUN (JAZM)

LESSON : 71

درس : ٧١

Pronunciation only to be taught.

صرف تلفظ بتایا جائے۔

ظِلُّ   لِكِنۡ   فِلُّ

مِلُّ فِلُّ ظِلُّ كِنۡ مِنۡ اِنۡ فِلُّ بِشۡ

غِشُّ فِلُّ نِلُّ ضِلُّ

LESSON : 72

درس : ٧٢

Try to teach the child pronunciation only.

بچے کو صرف تلفظ سمجھانے کی کوشش کریں۔

تِلۡكَ رِزۡقَ اِذۡقَالَ سَبۡتِ صِدۡقِ اِنۡسٍ

ذِكۡرَ وِزۡرَ وِرۡثَ قِسۡطَ اِسۡمَ لَبِثۡتَ

LESSON : 73

درس : ٧٣

Pronunciation only should be taught.

صرف تلفظ بتائیں۔

حِفۡظَ صِدۡقَ اِنۡسَ مِلۡكَ عِلۡمَ رِفۡقَ مِثۡلَ

شِعۡرَ مِلۡتَ قَبِلۡتَ عَلِمۡتَ خِفۡتَ

35

LESSON : 74	مخلوط مشق	درس : ٧٤

MIXED EXERCISE

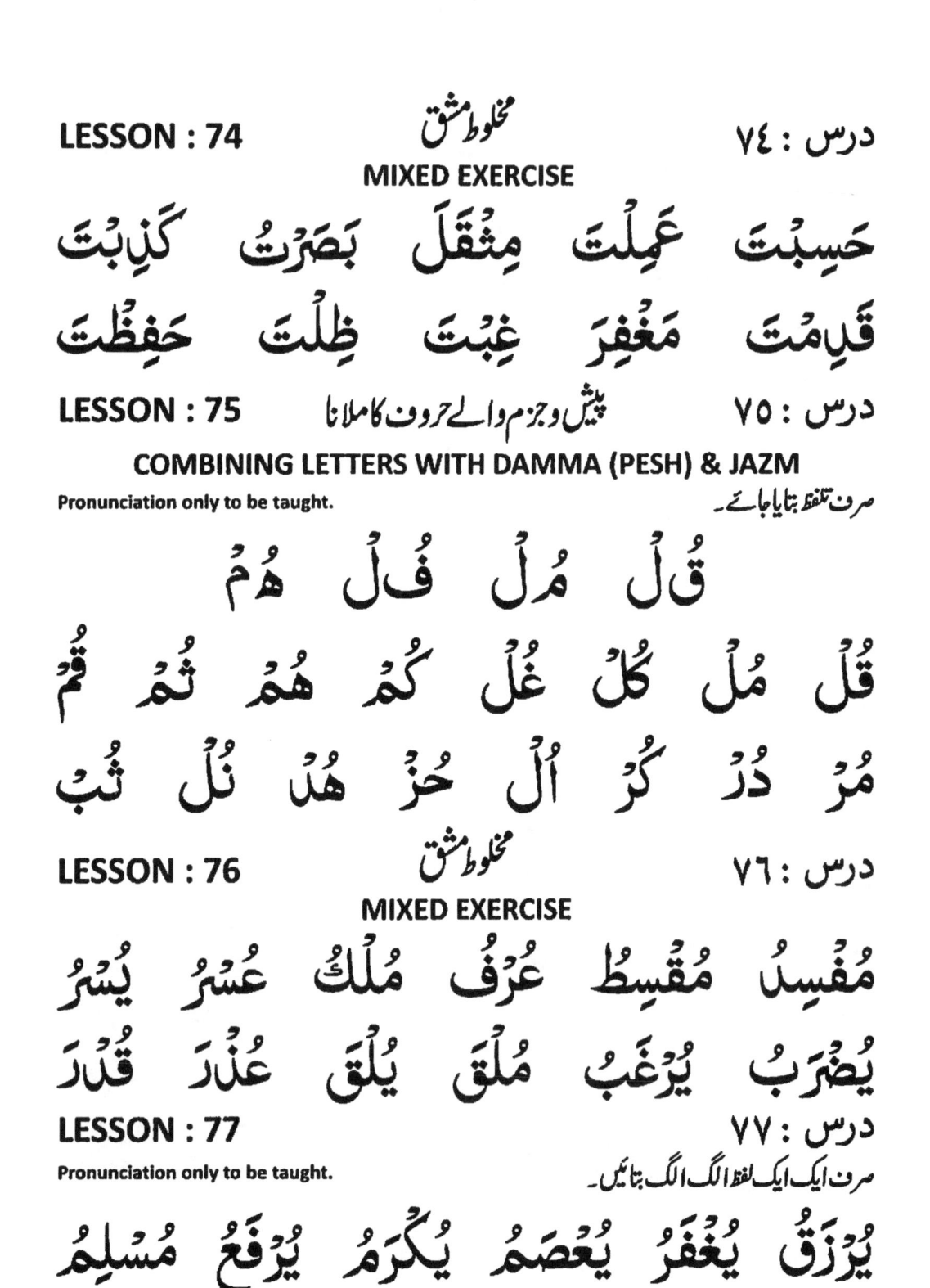

كَذِبَتْ بَصَرَتْ مِثْقَلْ عَمِلَتْ حَسِبَتْ

حَفِظَتْ ظِلَّتْ غِبَتْ مَغْفِرَ قَدِّمَتْ

LESSON : 75	پیش و جزم والے حروف کا ملانا	درس : ٧٥

COMBINING LETTERS WITH DAMMA (PESH) & JAZM

Pronunciation only to be taught.   صرف تلفظ بتایا جائے۔

هُمْ فُلْ مُلْ قُلْ

قُمْ ثُمْ هُمْ كُمْ غُلْ كُلْ مُلْ قُلْ

ثُبْ نُلْ هُدْ اُلْ حُزْ كُرْ دُرْ مُرْ

LESSON : 76	مخلوط مشق	درس : ٧٦

MIXED EXERCISE

يُسُرْ عُسْرْ مُلْكٌ عُرْفٌ مُقْسِطْ مُفْسِدٌ

قُدْرَ عُنْدَ يُلْقَ مُلْقَ يُرْغَبْ يُضْرَبْ

LESSON : 77		درس : ٧٧

Pronunciation only to be taught.   صرف ایک ایک لفظ الگ الگ بتائیں۔

مُسْلِمْ يُرْفَعْ يُكْرَمْ يُعْصَمْ يُغْفَرْ يُرْزَقُ

مُؤْمِن اَمْهِلْهُمْ اُنْظُرْ مُشْرِك مُجْرِمُ

LESSON : 78

درس : ۷۸

Words with mix vowel marks.
Teach each word separately.

مخلوط اعراب والے الفاظ ہر ایک لفظ الگ بتائیں۔

سَهَرَ فَضْلُ مَنْ يَرْزُقُ سُئِلَ يُغْفَرْ

يُعْرَفُ وَمَنْ كَفَرَ فُتِحَ لَهُمْ اَبْوَابُ يُظْلَمُ

مَنْ كَسَبَ فَاٰمَنَ فَدَخَلَ كَانَ عِنْدَكَ

LESSON : 79

درس : ۷۹

Pronunciation only to be taught.

صرف تلفظ بتایا جائے۔

مَنْ اَسْلَمَ فَقَدْ فَازَ وَلَقَدْ عَلِمْنَا جَعَلْنَا

اِنْ عُدْتُمْ مِنْ قَوْمِ فِرْعَوْنَ بَعَثْنَا اَنْ اَلْقِ

عَصَاكَ فَاِذَا هِيَ تَلْقَفُ بِمَا اُنْزِلَ اَلْحَمْدُ

نَعْبُدُ اِهْدِنَا رَزَقْنَا هُمْ ءَ اَنْذَرْتَهُمْ اَمْ لَمْ

تُنْذِرْهُمْ

LESSON : 80

Teach each word separately

ہر ایک لفظ جدا جدا بتایا جائے۔

كُمْ مِنْ صِرَاطَ اَنْعَمْتَ مِنْ قَبْلِكَ اَنْفُسَهُمْ

كَمَا اٰمَنَ لَذَهَبَ وَاَرِنَا مَنَاسِكَنَا نَحْنُ خَلَقْكُمْ

اِنْ كُنْتُمْ اَتَجْعَلُ بِحَمْدِكَ عَرَضَهُمْ لَا عِلْمَ

لَنَا فَزَادَهُمْ يَسْتَغْفِرُ وَلَا يُقْبَلُ مِنْهَا وَلَقَدْ

جَاءَتْ رُسُلُنَا مَنْ كَانَ عَمِلَ رِزْقُكُمْ

تنوین والے حروف کی مشق
EXERCISE OF LETTER WITH NUNATION (TANWIN)

بچے کو سمجھایا جائے کہ جزم کی بجائے دو زبر، دو زیر، دو پیش پڑھے جاتے ہیں۔ اور "بَنْ" کے نون مجزوم کو حذف کر کے صرف دو زبر ٓ، دو زیر ٍ، دو پیش ٌ کسی حرف پر پڑھے جائیں تو نون ساکن ظاہر ہو جائے گا۔ جیسے بَنْ سے بً۔ لیکن ن ساکن تنوین کے وقت پڑھا جاتا ہے اور لکھا نہیں جاتا۔

It should be explained to the child that instead of Sukun (Jazm), two Fatha (Zabar), two Kasra (Zer), two Damma (Pesh) are read, and replacing Nun with Sukun (Jazm) in 'Ban', if only two vowel marks (two Fatha, Kasra or Damma) are read, the Nun will become Sakin (Tanwin) at the end, e.g. from 'Ban'; but Nun (Sakin) with Tanwin is written and not read.

تنوین ً ٍ ٌ

LESSON : 81
Ask the child to identify.

درس : ۸۱
بچے سے شناخت کرائیں۔

دو زبر ﮐ ، دو زیر ﮐ ، دو پیش ﮐ ، دو زبر ﮐ ، دو زیر ﮐ ، دو پیش ﮐ

Let him spell it.

بچے کرائیں ب زبر نون بَنْ ء

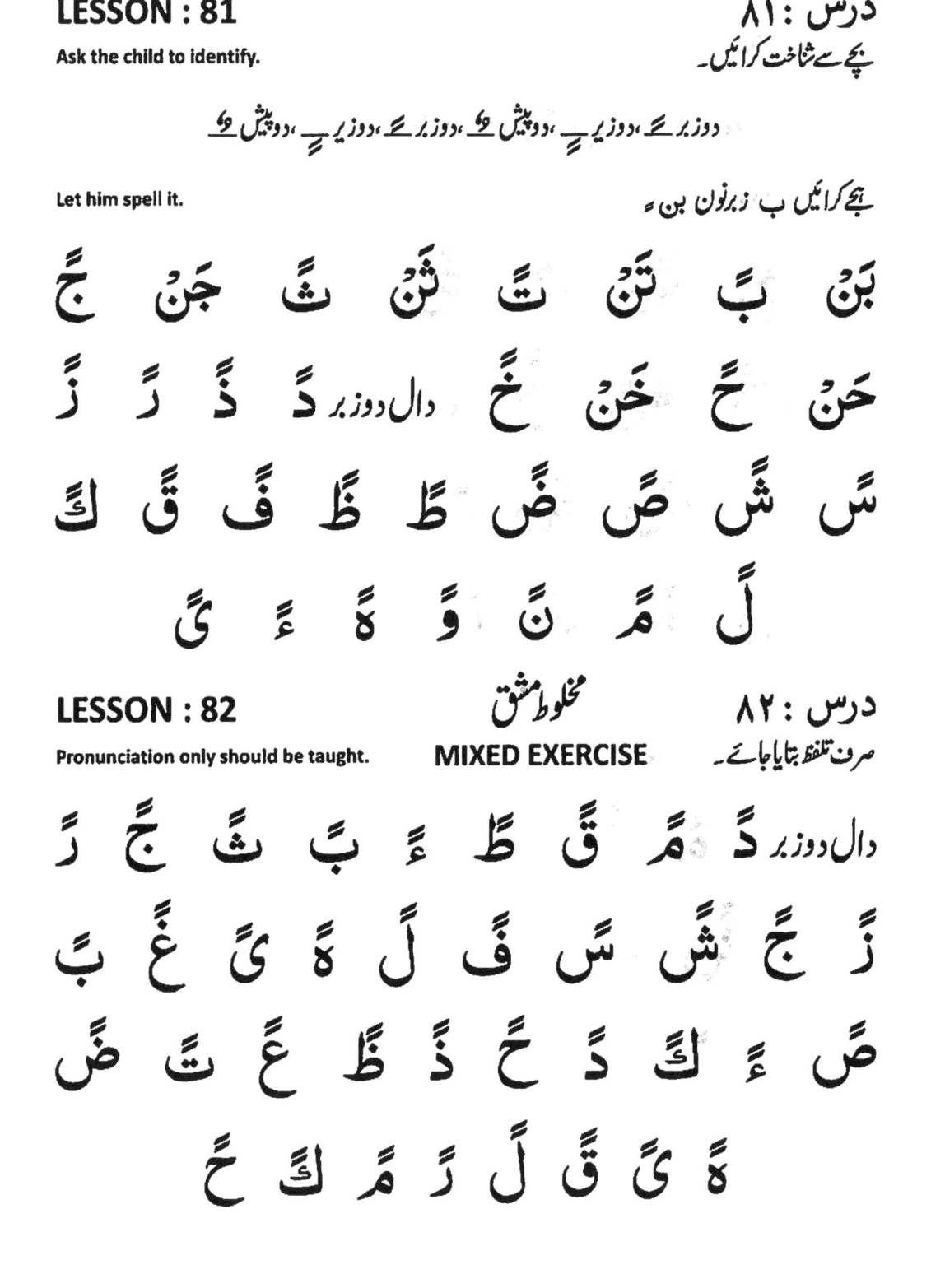

بَنْ بَ تَنْ تَ ثَنْ ثَ جَنْ جَ

حَنْ حَ خَنْ خَ دال دو زبر دَ ذَ رَ زَ

سَ شَ صَ ضَ طَ ظَ فَ قَ كَ

لَ مَ نَ وَ ہَ ءَ ئَ

LESSON : 82
Pronunciation only should be taught.

مخلوط مشق
MIXED EXERCISE

درس : ۸۲
صرف تلفظ بتایا جائے۔

دال دو زبر دَ مَّ قَ طَ ءَ بَ ثَّ جَّ رَ

رَّ جَّ شَّ سَّ فَ لَ ہَ ئَ غَّ بَ

صَّ ءَ كَ دَ حَّ ذَّ ظَّ عَّ تَّ ضَّ

ہَ ئَ قَ لَ رَّ مَّ كَ حَّ

دو زیر والے حروف کی مشق کیلئے بچے کرانے کی ضرورت ہے۔

EXERCISE OF LETTERS WITH KASRATAIN (TWO ZERS) NEEDS TO BE SPELLED OUT

LESSON : 83

درس : ٨٣

بے زیر نون بِن بِ تِن تِ تِن تِ ثِ جِن جِ

جِ دِ ذِ رِ زِ سِ شِ صِ ضِ طِ

ظِ عِ غِ فِ قِ کِ لِ مِ نِ

وِ ہِ ءِ یِ

مخلوط حروف کی مشق

EXERCISE OF MIXED LETTERS

LESSON : 84

درس : ٨٤

Spellings should be done

بچے کرائے جائیں۔

ر دوزیر لِ نِ بِ بِ خِ جِ دِ ثِ

حِ شِ ضِ ظِ غِ کِ قِ فِ

ہِ بِ ءِ یِ صِ عِ مِ تِ

زِ لِ ذِ وِ طِ فِ لِ جِ

و٘

دو پیش والے حروف کی مشق

EXERCISE OF LETTERS WITH DAMMATAIN (TWO PESHS)

LESSON : 85

درس : ٨٥

Spellings to be made.

ب پیش نون بُن ہجے کرائے جائیں۔

بُن بٌ تُن تٌ ثُن ثٌ جُن جٌ

د دوپیش دُ دٌ رُ رٌ سُ سٌ شٌ صٌ

ضٌ طٌ ظُ ظٌ عُ غٌ فٌ قٌ کٌ

مخلوط حرفوں کی مشق

EXERCISE OF MIXED LETTERS

LESSON : 86

درس : ٨٦

دٌ مُ سٌ شٌ ضٌ غٌ لُ ذٌ رُ

رٌ بٌ نٌ قٌ جٌ حُ مُ دُ ہٌ

خُ ءٌ ئٌ عُ فٌ طٌ ظٌ کٌ وُ

42

تَنْوِین والے مرکب حرفوں کی مشق

EXERCISE OF COMPOUND LETTERS WITH NUNATION (TANWIN)

LESSON : 87

درس : ۸۷

Pronunciation only to be taught.

صرف تلفظ بتایا جائے۔

غَرِبٍ غَرَقٍ خُلُقٍ مِلَكٍ حِزْبٍ بٍ

قَطِرٍ مَطِرٍ قَرْضٍ اَرْضٍ ضُعْفٍ حَرْبٍ

سَمَكٍ دَرَكٍ مَكْرٍ شُكْرٍ رِزْقٍ بَرْقٍ

كُفْرٍ عَنَبٍ اَلْفٍ حَرْفٍ فَجْرٍ بَقَرٍ

LESSON : 88

درس : ۸۸

جَهْرٌ اَمْرٌ فُلْكٌ مُلْكٌ حِلْمٌ عِلْمٌ مٌ

سَقْفٌ فِسْقٌ رِزْقٌ بَرْقٌ بَدَارٌ شَجَرٌ

كُرَةٌ مَرَضٌ خُلُّ عَدَدٌ عَبْدٌ حَمْلٌ

قَدَرٌ عَنَبٌ اَبَدٌ فَضْلٌ قَتْلٌ وَجْهٌ

43

LESSON : 89   درس : ٨٩

رً اَجْرًا اَمْرًا اَرْضًا قَرْضًا شَهَادَةً مَآءً

صَدَقَةً عَطَآءً عِشَآءً صَالِحًا عَالِمًا ظَالِمًا

قَائِلًا عَامِلًا حَاكِمًا عَازِمًا فَاجِرًا نَاصِرًا

خَالِقًا غَافِرًا جَابِرًا تَائِبًا غَالِبًا دَافِعًا

شَهْرٍ فَجْرٍ نَشْطًا قَدْحًا فَضْلٌ قَمَرٌ

شِقَاقٍ اَشْتَاتًا غِشَاوَةٌ فَاكِهَةٌ خَاطِئَةٍ

وجزی تختی کی مشق

EXERCISE OF 'WAU WITH SUKUN (JAZM)

ہدایت: اس مشق میں بچے کو واؤ ساکن اور ماقبل مضموم کو پڑھنے کا طریقہ بتایا جائے۔ مگر شروع میں دو تین حرفوں کے بچے کرائے جائیں، باقی روواں پڑھے۔ نیز بچے کو یہ بھی اچھی طرح ذہن نشین کرا دیا جائے کہ جس حرف پر الٹا پیش ہو وہ بھی واؤ والے پیش کی طرح آواز دے گا۔ جیسے اُو وُ ءُ

In this exercise, the child should be taught the method of reading 'Wau' (sakin) with a letter with Damma (Pesh) on it. The first two or three words should be spelled out and the rest to be read fluently. He should also be explained that an inverted Damma (Pesh) is also pronounced as 'Wau'. e.g. 'Hu', 'Wu', 'Uu'.

LESSON : 90   درس : ٩٠

ا پیش و اُو   ب پیش و بُو   ت پیش و تُو

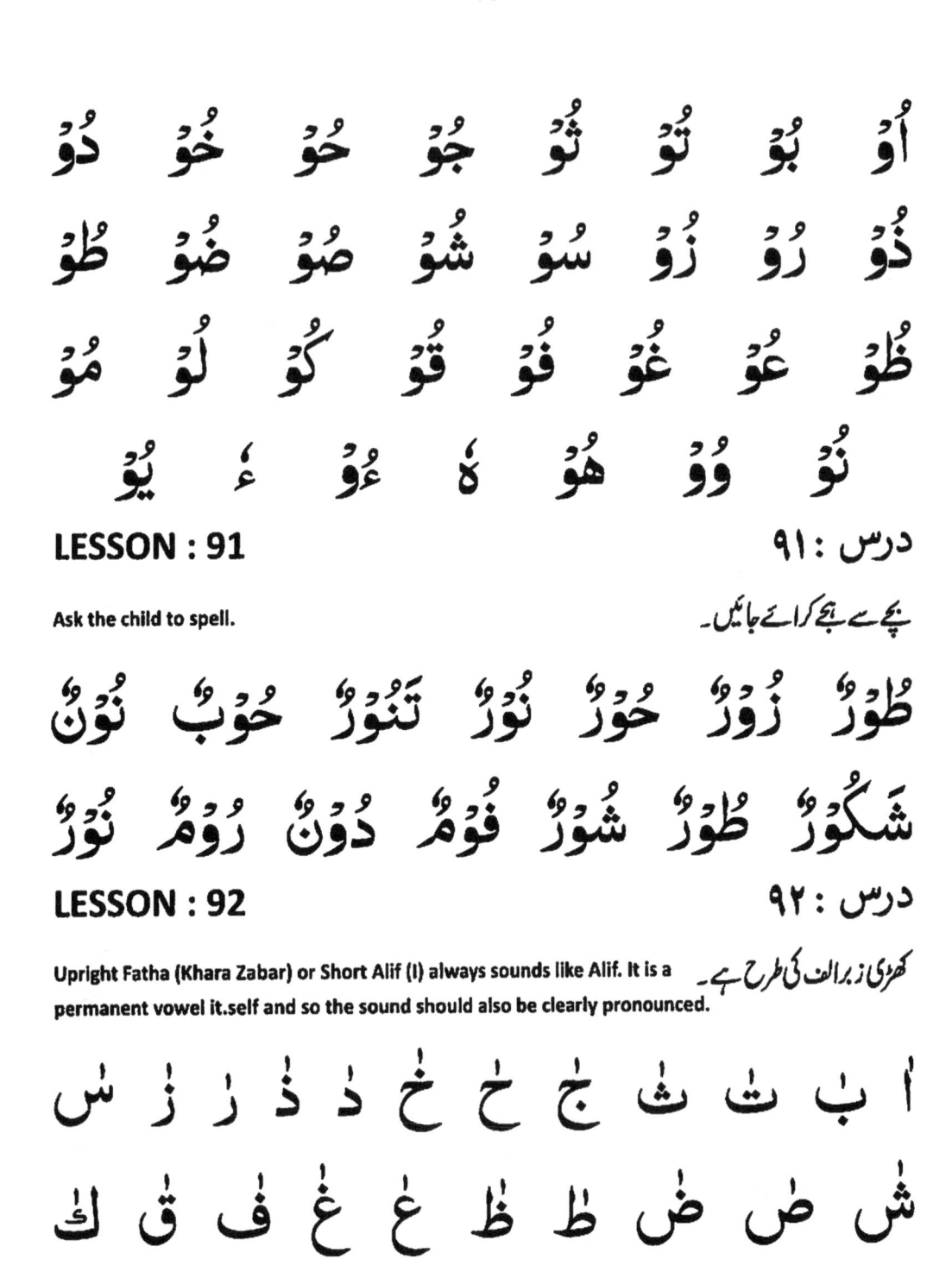

دُو خُو حُو جُو ثُو تُو بُو اُو

طُو ضُو صُو شُو سُو زُو رُو ذُو

مُو لُو کُو قُو فُو غُو عُو ظُو

يُو ءُ اُو ہ ھُو وُو نُو

LESSON : 91

درس : ۹۱

Ask the child to spell.

بچے سے ہجے کرائے جائیں۔

نُونْ حُوبْ تَنُورْ نُورْ حُورْ زُورْ طُورْ

نُورْ رُومْ دُونْ فُومْ شُورْ طُورْ شَکُورْ

LESSON : 92

درس : ۹۲

Upright Fatha (Khara Zabar) or Short Alif (I) always sounds like Alif. It is a permanent vowel it.self and so the sound should also be clearly pronounced.

کھڑی زبر الف کی طرح ہے۔

سْ رْ ذْ دْ خْ حْ جْ ثْ تْ بْ اْ

كْ قْ فْ غْ عْ ظْ طْ ضْ صْ شْ

ئْ ءْ ھْ وْ نْ مْ لْ كْ

قَالَ قُلْ مَالِكِ مَلِكِ اٰدَمَ اٰمَنَ كِتٰبْ

سَمٰوٰتِ مَلٰئِكَةِ خَطٰيٰكُمْ ذٰلِكَ يٰبَنِيْ

كَلِمٰتِ اٰمَنْتُ

LESSON : 93 درس : ٩٣

غَفُوْرٌ شَكُوْرٌ رَءُوْفٌ اَلُوْفٌ يَئُوْسٌ قُبُوْلْ

مَعْلُوْمٌ ذَلُوْلٌ مَلْعُوْنٌ نَصُوْحٌ وَدُوْدٌ وَرُوْدٌ

عَجُوْلٌ حُضُوْرٌ زُوْرٌ طَهُوْرٌ قُصُوْرٌ عُوْدٌ

اٰمِنُوْا اَذِنُوْا اَحْسَنُوْا عَمِلُوْا دَخَلُوْا نُوْرٌ

عَزَمُوْا هَزَمُوْا وَلَجُوْا خَرَجُوْا بَرَزُوْا

حَرَزُوْا فَرَغُوْا بَلَغُوْا عَرَفُوْا وَصَفُوْا

وجزی تختی کی مشق۔

EXERCISE OF LETTERS WITH 'WAU' AND SUKUN (JAZM)

LESSON : 94 درس : ٩٤

The child should read easily. بچہ روال پڑھے۔

يَدْخُلُوْنَ يَعْمَلُوْنَ نَصِرُوْنَ نٰظِرُوْنَ

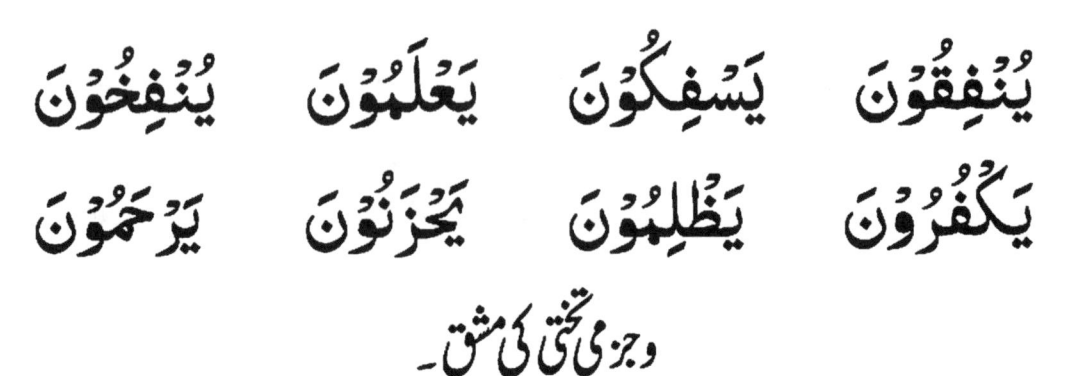

وجزی تختی کی مشق۔

EXERCISE OF 'WAU' WITH SUKUN (JAZM)

LESSON : 95		**۹۵ : درس**

مندرجہ ذیل مشق بچے کو دو تین حروف کے ہجے کرانے کے بعد روال پڑھائیں۔

The following exercise should be read easily, after spelling first two or three words.

تَوْ ت زبر و بَوْ ب زبر و اَوْ از بر او

دَوْ خُوْ حَوْ جَوْ ثُوْ تَوْ بَوْ اَوْ

طَوْ ضَوْ صَوْ شَوْ سَوْ زَوْ رَوْ ذَوْ

مَوْ لَوْ کَوْ قَوْ فَوْ غَوْ عَوْ ظَوْ

یَوْ ءَوْ وَوْ نَوْ

وجزی تختی کی مشق۔

EXERCISE OF 'WAU' WITH SUKUN (JAZM)

LESSON : 96		**۹۶: درس**

بچہ روال پڑھے۔

The child should read easily.

قَوْلٌ حَوْلٌ طَوْلٌ ثَوْرٌ غَوْرٌ لَوْمٌ طَوْرٌ غَوْلٌ

لَوْحٌ فَوْزٌ حَوْضٌ رَوْضٌ خَوْضٌ مَوْتٌ فَوْتٌ

مَوْجٌ فَوْجٌ خَوْفٌ زَوْجٌ قَوْمٌ يَوْمٌ

وجزی تختی کی مشق ۔

EXERCISE OF 'WAU' WITH SUKUN (JAZM)

LESSON : 97

درس : ۹۷

بچہ روال پڑھے ۔

Child to read easily.

فَمَضَوْا وَرَمَوْا وَإِذَاخَلَوْا مَوْرِدٌ مَوْعِدٌ

خَلَوْنَ اِذَاَوَيْنَا اٰمَنُوْا فَاَبَوْا يَوْمَ تَرَوْنَهَا

وَشَرَوْا وَيَرَوْنَ يَوْمَئِذٍ اَوْلَادِكُمْ اِلٰى قَوْمٍ

وجزی تختی کی مشق ۔

EXERCISE OF 'WAU' WITH SUKUN (JAZM)

LESSON : 98

درس : ۹۸

بچے کو روال پڑھایا جائے ۔

Child should be taught easily.

اٰذَانِهِمْ يَدْخُلُوْنَ يَفْقَهُوْنَ جَهُوْلٌ قَوْلٌ

48

مَعْرُوْفٌ مِنْ صَدَقَةٍ يَسْتَغْفِرُوْنَ تَبُوْرُ

يُرْزَقُوْنَ قَوْلًا كَرِيْمًا وَقَالَ لَهُمْ وَلَوْ كَرِهَ

الْمُجْرِمُوْنَ

مخلوط مشق

LESSON : 99　　**MIXED EXERCISE**　　درس : ٩٩

يَلْعَبُوْنَ مُؤْمِنُوْنَ مُنْتَقِمُوْنَ كَسَبُوْا غَوْلٌ

قُبُوْرٌ مَنَافِعُ فِيْ صَلٰوتِهِمْ خَاشِعُوْنَ اَلَآ لَهُ

الْاَمْرُ وَالْخَلْقُ قَالُوْا هٰذَا سِحْرٌ اَوْفُوْا

ی جزمی تحتی

EXERCISE OF YA' WITH SUKUN (JAZM)

اس جگہ لکھی ہوئی مشقوں کی ابتدائی ایک مشق کے بچے کو اچھی طرح سمجھا دینے چاہیئں، باقی تمام مشق کو رواں پڑھے۔ ساتھ ہی اس کو یہ سمجھا دیا جائے کہ جس حرف کے پیچھے الف کی طرح لمبی زبر لکھی ہوئی ہو تو وہ بھی ی کا کام دیتی ہے۔ جیسے
بہ نہ لہ

The spelling of the first of the following written exercises should be explained fully to the child. He should read the rest easily. He should also understand that an upright Kasra (Zer) below a letter also works as a 'Ya', e.g. 'Hi', Ni, Li.

49

LESSON : 100

He should spell the words.

درس : ۱۰۰

بچے کراۓ جائیں۔

تٖی تِی بٖی بٔی نٖی اٖی ی ازیر

دٖی خٖی جٖی جِی ثٖی تٖی بِی نٔی

طٖی ضٖی صٖی شٖی سٖی زٖی رٖی زٔی

مٖی لٖی کٖی فٖی قٖی غٖی عٖی ظٖی

پٔی نٔی ۀ ھٖی ؤی نٖی

LESSON : 101

مخلوط مشق

MIXED EXERCISE

درس : ۱۰۱

نٖی قٖی غٖی طٖی سٖی لٖی دٖی جٖی

بٖیْتَ بٖیْبَ غٖیْبَ مٖیْثَ لٖیْبَ دٖیْبَ حٖیْفَ جٖیْفَ

غَرٖیْبٌ شَرٖیْفٌ عَزٖیْزٌ دَلٖیْلٌ طٖیْبٌ سٖیْرَ

فَرٖیْقٌ حَرٖیْصٌ کَبٖیْرٌ فَقٖیْرٌ حَمٖیْدٌ رَشٖیْدٌ

LESSON : 102

Teach pronounci ation only.

صرف تلفظ بتایا جائے۔

زِیْ کِیْ لِیْ بِیْ نِیْ رِیْ قِیْ فِیْ

فِیْلٌ قَلِیْلٌ اَنِیْسٌ مَرِیْضٌ خَبِیْرٌ دَلِیْلٌ قَدِیْرٌ

حَکِیْمٌ عَلِیْمٌ حَفِیْظٌ ذَلِیْلٌ نَصِیْرٌ عَظِیْمٌ

عَقِیْمٌ ظَهِیْرٌ مُرِیْدٌ حَمِیْمٌ رَحِیْمٌ

ی جزمی تختی کی مشق۔

LESSON : 103   EXERCISE OF 'YA' WITH SUKUN (JAZM)

The child should read easily.

بچے رو اں پڑھے۔

عَذَابِیْ بَدَالِیْ اَسَانِیْ کَمَانِیْ دَعَانِیْ اَمِرِیْ

جَانِیْ رَانِیْ کَافِیْ وَافِیْ بَاقِیْ صَافِیْ

رَامِیْ حَامِیْ قَاضِیْ کَلَامِیْ غُلَامِیْ اَهْلِیْ

بَعْلِیْ اَمِرِیْ

LESSON : 104

درس : ۱۰٤

بچہ روال پڑھے۔

The child should read easily.

نَبِیْ وَلِیْ اَبِیْ اَخِیْ مَاضِیْ قَاضِیْ رَاضِیْ

حَیَاتِیْ مَمَاتِیْ عَذَابِیْ کِتَابِیْ اٰیَاتِیْ مَلَائِکَتِیْ

کُرْسِیْ اَرْضِیْ اَمْرِیْ اَرْزِیْ هَبْ لِیْ عِیْشَتِیْ

LESSON : 105

درس : ۱۰۵

کھڑی زیر یا کی طرح ہے۔

Upright Kasra (Khari Zer) sounds exactly like 'Ya' or 'Ya'i Ma'ruf'.

ا ب ت ث ج ح خ د ذ ر ز س

ش ص ض ط ظ ع غ ف ق ك

گ ل م ن و ه ء ی

بِهٖ یُحْیٖ اِبْرَاهٖمَ اِلْفِهٖمْ وَقِیْلِهٖ بَعْدِهٖ

LESSON : 106

درس : ۱۰٦

بچہ روال پڑھے۔

Child should read easily.

بِهٖ هٰذِهٖ فِیْ مَالِهٖ فِیْ مُلْکِهٖ فِیْ اَرْضِهٖ لِنَفْسِهٖ

لِرَبِّهٖ لِحَزْمِهٖ فِیْ وَجْهَهٖ لِحُکْمِهٖ وَلِعَبْدِهٖ لَا

يَنْبَغِيْ وَلَهُمْ فِيْهَا وَ مَنْ لَقِيَنِيْ وَ مَنْ رَاٰنِيْ

يَهْتَدِيْ يَهْدِيْ بَلَغَنِيْ مُنَادٍ يُنَادِيْ اِيْمَانٌ

عِبَادِيْ اَمَرَنِيْ بِقَلْبٍ سَلِيْمٍ وَ مَنْ اَعْرَضَ عَنْ

ذِكْرِيْ مَعِيْشَةً ضَنْكًا مُسْلِمِيْنَ وَارِثِيْنَ

خَالِدِيْنَ فِيْهَا تَجْرِيْ

زبر والے حروف کے ساتھ یائے ساکن کا ملانا

COMBINING LETTERS HAVING FATHA (ZABAR) WITH 'YA'

LESSON : 107 درس : ۱۰۷

بَيْ تَيْ ثَيْ جَيْ حَيْ خَيْ دَيْ ذَيْ

رَيْ زَيْ سَيْ شَيْ صَيْ ضَيْ طَيْ ظَيْ

عَيْ غَيْ فَيْ قَيْ كَيْ لَيْ مَيْ نَيْ

وَيْ هَيْ ءَيْ يَيْ

ی جزمی تختی کی مشق۔

EXERCISE OF 'YA' WITH SUKUN (JAZM)

ھدایت : بچے کو سمجھا دیا جائے کہ ی سے پہلے حرف پر اگر زبر ہو تو اس طرح پڑھنا ہوگا ۔ الف زبر یائی اَیْ
اسی طرح شروع میں تھوڑے سے ہجے پڑھانے کے بعد پھر رواں پڑھے ۔

It should be explained to the child that a Fatha (Zabar) on a letter before 'Ya' should be read like this: Alif Zabar Ya, Ay. Similarly start with few spellings and then he should read easily.

LESSON : 108

درس : ۱۰۸

Let him spell.

ہجے کرائے جائیں ۔

ثَیْ   شَیْ   تَیْ   بَیْ   بَیْ   اَیْ

قَیْ   سَیْ   رَیْ   مَیْ   نَیْ   اَیْ   جَیْ   جَیْ

سَمَیْ   قَضَیْ   لَکَیْ   ھَدَیْ   فَدَیْ   رَمَیْ   لَقَیْ

فَیْض   خَیْط   غَیْر   رَیْب   اٰتَیْن   دَیْن   اَیْن

LESSON : 109

درس : ۱۰۹

اٰیْمَان   مُسْلِمَیْنِ   یَرْضَیْن   اُخْتَیْن   اَلْفَیْن   اٰتَیْن

اَمِیْنٌ   بَلٌّ   جَبَلَیْنِ   مَلَکَیْنِ   ھَدَیْن   ھَوَیْن

غُلَامَیْنِ   یَتِیْمَیْن   فَرِیْقَیْنِ   کَامِلَیْنِ   فِیْ بَیْتِہٖ

وَقِیْلَ   لِکَیْلَا   اِلَیْكَ

LESSON : 110

The child should read easily.

درس : ١١٠

بچہ روانی سے پڑھے۔

عَزِيْزٌ حَكِيْمٌ قَالَ لِاَبِيْهِ عَابِدِيْنَ شَاكِرِيْنَ
اَمْرِىْ اِلَيْكَ وَ لَمْ يَمْسَسْنِىْ عَذَابِىْ لَشَدِيْدٌ قَدْ
كَانَ فِيْهِمْ لَيْسَ لَكَ شَرِيْكٌ فِى الْمُلْكِ
وَ اٰتَيْنَاهُمْ كِتَابًا وَ اِلَيْهِ الْمَاٰبُ

مخلوط مشقیں

MIXED EXERCISES

LESSON : 111

درس : ١١١

وَ مَنْ دَخَلَ كَانَ اٰمِنًا وَ ذٰلِكَ دِيْنٌ لَا رَيْبَ فِيْهِ
فِيْهَا سُرُرٌ مَرْفُوْعَةٌ وَّاَكْوَابٌ مَوْضُوْعَةٌ وَ هُوَ
الْعَزِيْزُ الْحَمِيْدُ كُلُوْا وَاشْرَبُوْا وَلَا تَحْزَنُوْا
وَ اَنْتُمُ الْاَعْلَوْنَ

LESSON : 112

درس : ١١٢

لَا تَسْئَلُوْا عَنْ اَشْيَاءَ وَاشْكُرُوْا لَهٗ وَ مَنْ عَمِلَ
عَمَلًا صَالِحًا غَيْرِ الْمَغْضُوْبِ اِهْدِنَا

LESSON : 113

Inverted Damma (Ulti Pesh) replaces a 'Wau' and sounds like it.

الٹی پیش واؤ کی طرح ہے۔

اُ بُ تُ ثُ جُ حُ خُ دُ ذُ رُ زُ سُ

شُ صُ ضُ طُ ظُ عُ غُ فُ قُ كُ

كُ لُ مُ نُ وُ ہُ ءُ ئُ

لَهُ نَهُ دَاوُدَ جَالُوتَ سُبْحٰنَهُ

اٰخْرَجَهُ اٰمَرَهُ وَجْهَهُ

LESSON : 114

كَفَرُوا سَوَاءٌ عَلَيْهِمْ فِي قُلُوبِهِمْ مَرَضٌ لَا

تُفْسِدُوا فِي الْاَرْضِ وَاِذَا خَلَوْا اِلٰى شَيَاطِينِهِمْ

يَقُولُونَ لَيْسَ عَلَيْهِ جُنَاحٌ غَيْرَ بَاغٍ فَاعْتَصِمُوا

قُومُوا هٰذِهٖ

مَدّ والی تختی کی مشق

EXERCISES OF LETTERS WITH MADD (PROLONGATION MARK)

56

بڑی مد آ چھوٹی مد آ
SHORT MADD   LONG MADD

ہدایات : بچے کو بتایا جائے کہ جس حرف پر ان دو شکلوں میں سے کوئی شکل لکھی ہوئی ہو تو اس حرف کے زیر، زبر، پیش کو کھینچ کر پڑھنا ہو گا۔ اگر بڑی مد " ـٓ " ہو گی تو کافی زیادہ کھینچ کر تلفظ ادا کیا جائے گا۔ اگر چھوٹی مد " ـٓ " ہو گی تو تھوڑا کم۔ پہلے خود تلفظ کو ادا کر کے بچے کو سنایا جائے۔

The child should be told that any letter which carries one of the above marks (of Madda) over it, Fatha (Zabar), Kasra (Zer), Damma (Pesh) of this letter should be prolonged (stretched). If it is a long Madda, it will be prolonged more, and if it is a short Madda, a little less. You should pronounce it first for the child to hear it, and learn it.

LESSON : 115
درس : ۱۱۵

Exercise of Long Madda

بڑی مد کی مشق

عَلٰى نِسَآءِ الْعَالَمِيْن يَابَنِىْ اِسْرَآءِيْلَ الٓمٓ

اِلٰى كَلِمَةٍ سَوَآءٍ قَآئِمًا اُولٰٓئِكَ وَجَآءَهُمْ ضِيَآءٌ

قَآئِمِيْن طَآئِفِيْن دِمَآؤُهُمْ حُنَفَآءَ شَعَآئِرَ

سَمَآءٌ شُهَدَآءُ

LESSON : 116
درس : ۱۱۶

Exercise of Short Madda.

چھوٹی مد کی مشق

قَضٰى مُوْسٰى يِعِيْسٰى عَلٰى اَزْوَاجِهِمْ مَا هٰذَآ

مَاۤ اَتَوۡا قَالُوۡا ءَاِذَا مِتۡنَا لَا اِلٰهَ فِيۡهَا مَا كَانُوۡا
كَمَا لَوۡ لَاۤ سَتَجِدُنِیۤ عَجِبُوۡا اَنۡزَلۡنَاۤ

نوشتہ کی تختی کی مشق

EXERCISE OF LETTERS WITH NINE TYPES OF SHADD

شدّ ''لّا''

SHADD (DOUBLING OF LETTERS)

ہدایات : بچے کو سمجھایا جائے کہ تین دندانے والی شکل کو شد کہتے ہیں ۔ اس کا کام صرف یہ
ہے کہ دو حرفوں کو اکٹھا باندھ دینا یعنی باہم ملا دینا ہے ۔ یہ نو طرح سے استعمال ہوتی ہے ۔

نیز نیچے لکھی ہوئی مشق سے بچے کو شد ، زبر ، زیر بتائیں ۔

It should be explained to the child that the mark with three teeth is called 'Shadd.' It is used
to bind two letters together, i.e. combine them (strengthen them). It is used in nine different
ways. Also from the exercise below, teach the child Shadd, Fatha (Zabar), Kasra (Zer), etc.

لّاُ لّاُ لّاَ لّاِ لّاُ لّاَ لّاَ

لّاُ لّاَ لّاَ لّاُ لّاِ لّاَ لّاُ

Lesson: 117

درس : ۱۱۷

Let the child should read easily.

بچہ روانی پڑھے

اَدّ حَلّ جَلّ وَدّ حَجّ ضَلّ قَلّ عَفّ
عَزّ مَنّ حَقّ عَضّ اَوّ عَمّ شَفّ عَلّ
شَتّ اَنّ بَثّ خَفّ اَیّ

LESSON : 118
The child should read easily.

درس : ۱۱۸
بچے روال پڑے۔

رَبَّ سَبَّ عَلَّ حَلَّ مَلَّ فَرَّ ضَرَّ كَرَّ

حَرَّ مَرَّ جَدَّ رَدَّ فَدَّ بَلَّ قَلَّ جَلَّ

ذَلَّ ظَلَّ قَصَّ مَنَّ غَصَّ شَدَّ حَدَّ لَدَّ

دَسَّ عَسَّ حَبَّ صَبَّ

LESSON : 119
The child should read easily.

درس : ۱۱۹
بچے روال پڑے۔

رَبُّكَ حَرَّمَ اَنَّكَ سَبَّحَ جَدَّكَ مِمَّا اِلَّا

اِنَّكَ بِاللهِ لِلّهِ اُمَّةً حُجَّةً مِلَّةً لٰكِنَّهُ

عِزَّةً اِنَّهُ قَرَّبَهُ قَبَّلَهُ عَذَّبَهُ عَدَّدَهُ مِنَّا

LESSON : 120

درس : ۱۲۰

مَكَّنَّهُ لِلّهِ عَجِّلَ اَوَّلُ تَقَبَّلَ اَضَلَّ اِيَّاكَ

حَيَّكَ سَوَّكَ سَخَّرَ فَسَّرَ حَذَّرَ قَدَّرَ تَوَّابُ

اُذُنٌ وَ حُزْنٌ وَ اَرْضٌ وَ مُلْكٌ وَ خُلُقٌ وَ

LESSON : 121

درس : ۱۲۱

بچے کو صرف تلفظ بتایا جائے ۔ اِدغام کے ساتھ پڑھا جائے یعنی ناک میں ۔

The child should be taught pronunciation only. He should read with 'Idgham', i.e. in the nose.

اَجْرٌ مِّنْ   نَصْرٌ مِّنْ   فَرِیْقٌ مِّنْ   حَرْبٌ مِّنْ

اِنْسٌ وَّلَاجَآنٌّ   کَرِیْمٍ وَّمَاهُوَ   تَنْزِیْلٌ مِّنْ   عَزِیْزٌ مِّنْ

LESSON : 122

درس : ۱۲۲

عَلِیْمٌ بِذَاتِ الصُّدُوْرِ   قَلِیْلًا مَّا تُؤْمِنُوْنَ   اِنَّهُ کُلٌّ

یَّجْرِیْ مِنْ رَّوْحِ اللهِ   سَارِبٌ بِالنَّهَارِ

۱۲۳

LESSON : 123

درس :

بچہ روال پڑھے ۔

The child should read easily.

خَوْفًا وَّ طَمَعًا وَّ جَنَّتٌ مِّنْ اَعْنَابٍ وَّزَرْعٌ وَّ نَخِیْلٌ

سِرًّا وَّ عَلَانِیَةً مِّنْ قَبْلِ کُلُّ نَفْسٍ مَّا کَسَبَتْ

LESSON : 124

درس : ۱۲٤

بچے کو تلفظ بتایا جائے ۔

The child should be taught pronunciation.

ضَآلُّوْنَ   مَآدُّوْنَ   حَآجُّوْنَ   اَلْحَآقَّةُ   کَآفَّةٌ

60

دَآبَّةٌ مُدَّهَآمَّتٰنِ اَيُكُمْ اَيَّانَ اَيُّهُمْ اَيْنَا

فِى الْاَيَّامِ الْخَالِيَةِ

مخلوط مشق

LESSON : 125 درس : ۱۲۵

يٰٓاَيُّهَا الَّذِيْنَ فَلَمَّا جَآءَهُمْ مُّوْسٰى اِنِّيْ اٰنَسْتُ

نَارًا لَّعَلِّيْ تَهْتَزُّ كَاَنَّهَا جَآنٌّ وَّلّٰى غَيْرَ سُوْءٍ وَّاضْمُمْ

رَبِّيْ اَعْلَمُ اِنَّهٗ لَا يُفْلِحُ الظّٰلِمُوْنَ لَعَلَّهُمْ يَتَذَكَّرُوْنَ

LESSON : 126 درس : ۱۲۶

The child should read easily.
بچہ روال پڑھے۔

يَبْسُطُ الرِّزْقَ لِمَنْ يَّشَآءُ مِنْ رَّبِّكَ كُلُّ شَيْئٍ وَمَنْ

جَآءَ بِالسَّيِّئَةِ اِنَّ الَّذِيْ اِنَّا كُنَّا نَصُرُّ مِنْ رَّبِّكَ

فِيْ ذُرِّيَّتِهِ النُّبُوَّةَ خَلَقَ اللهُ السَّمٰوٰتِ

LESSON : 127 درس : ۱۲۷

اٰيٰتٍ بَيِّنٰتٍ اِنَّ جَهَنَّمَ صَفَّتٍ وَالنّٰشِرٰتِ

وَالسّٰبِقٰتِ

وَالْمُدَبِّرَاتِ جَنَّةً وَّ حَرِيرًا الْحَمْدُ لِلّٰهِ رَبِّ الْعٰلَمِيْنَ الرَّحْمٰنِ الرَّحِيْمِ مٰلِكِ يَوْمِ الدِّيْنِ

LESSON : 128   درس : ۱۲۸

بچہ روال پڑے۔

The child should read easily.

صَوَّرَكُمْ سَخَّرَ لَكُمْ كَلَّا بَلْ تُحِبُّوْنَ قَدَّمَ وَ اٰخَّرَ وَالْتَفَّتِ السَّاقُ بِالسَّاقِ فَلَا صَدَّقَ وَلَا صَلّٰى وَلٰكِنْ كَذَّبَ وَتَوَلّٰى نُطْفَةً مِّنْ مَّنِيٍّ يُّمْنٰى بِالنَّفْسِ اللَّوَّامَةِ

LESSON : 129   درس : ۱۲۹

مُتَّكِئِيْنَ فِيْهَا عَلَى الْاَرَآئِكِ بِاٰنِيَةٍ مِّنْ فِضَّةٍ وَّالظّٰلِمِيْنَ اَعَدَّ لَهُمْ وَيْلٌ يَّوْمَئِذٍ لِّلْمُكَذِّبِيْنَ مِنْ مَّآءٍ مَّهِيْنٍ ذٰلِكَ الْيَوْمُ الْحَقُّ اِذَا السَّمَآءُ انْشَقَّتْ هَلْ ثُوِّبَ الْكُفَّارُ

کھڑی زبر کی مشق

EXERCISE OF LETTERS WITH UPRIGHT FATHA (ZABAR)

LESSON : 130 درس: ١٣٠

فَهُوَ يَرٰى مُوْسٰى عِيْسٰى هُدًى بِالتَّقْوٰى اِلٰى رَبِّكَ

الرُّجْعٰى وَ تَوَلّٰى اِذَا صَلّٰى خَيْرٌ لَّكَ مِنَ الْاُوْلٰى

وَالضُّحٰى وَالَّيْلِ اِذَا سَجٰى رَبُّكَ فَتَرْضٰى فَاٰوٰى تُجْزٰى

LESSON : 131   MIXED EXERCISE   درس: ١٣١

هٰذَا مِنْ فَضْلِ رَبِّيْ لَوْ كَانَ فِيْهِمَا لَاۤ اِلٰهَ اِلَّا

هُوَ وَالشَّمْسِ وَالْقَمَرِ لَا تَقْصُصْ رُءْيَاكَ قَالَ قَآئِلٌ

مِنْهُمْ لَا تَقْتُلُوْا يُوْسُفَ اِنَّكِ كُنْتِ مِنَ الْخٰطِئِيْنَ

LESSON : 132   درس: ١٣٢

Whenever a Sukun (Jazm) is followed by Shadd (together) the Jazm will be silent.

مِنْ يَّوْمٍ مِنْ مَّآءٍ قُلْ رَّبِّ مَهَّدْتَّ اَحَطْتَّ

عَبَدْتُّمْ يَكُنْ لَّهُنَّ مِنْ وَّرَآئِهِمْ اِرْكَبْ مَّعَنَا

وقف کرنا (ٹھہر جانا)

LESSON : 133 — MAKING A STOP (PAUSE) — درس : ۱۳۳

بچے کو سمجھائیں کہ جس حرف کے نیچے کی نشانیوں میں سے کوئی نشانی آ جائے اور وہ حرف حرکت والا ہو تو اسکے زیر یا زبر یا پیش کو کالعدم سمجھ کر اس کے ساتھ اسکے پہلے حرف کو ملا کر ساکن کر دیں اگر متحرک نہیں بلکہ اس پر جزم ہے تو وہ وہی صورت رہے گی۔ گول تے ہے سے بدل جائے گی۔ لمبی تے ہے سے نہیں بدلے گی۔ دو زبر کے بعد جو خالی الف ہے وہ پڑھا جائے گا۔ اور صرف ایک زبر پڑھا جائے گا۔ اگر الف سے پہلے ایک زبر ہے تو وہ وہی صورت رہے گی۔ دو زبر کے بعد خالی یے الف سے بدل جائے گی۔ باریک قلم سے ہر ایک کی مثال کے نیچے اس کا تلفظ درج کیا گیا ہے۔

It should be explained to the child that a letter followed by any of the following signs, with a vowel mark, should be make Sakin after joining it with the letter before it (dropping vowel marks). If there are no vowel marks, and is a Sakun (Jazm), it will remain the same. Round 'Ta' will be replaced by 'Ha'. Long 'Ta' will not be replaced by 'Ha'. Lone Alif, after two Fatha (Zabar) will be read, but only as if it had one Fatha (Zabar). will change into an Alif. In smaller type, the pronunciations of each example has been written below it.

علامت وقف مطلق ط	علامت وقف جائز ج	علامت وقف لازم م	علامت آیت ○
دَلْوَةٌ	لَهَبٍ	غَيْرَهُ	رُسُلِ
دَلْوَةٌ	لَهَبْ	غَيْرَهْ	رُسُلْ
عَظِيمٌ	صِدِّيقِينَ	فَنَسِيَهَا	هُوَ
عَظِيمْ	صِدِّيقِينْ	فَنَسِيَهْ	هُوْ
شَكُورٌ	تَعْلَمُونَ	يُنْفِقُونَ	شَيْءٍ
شَكُورْ	تَعْلَمُونْ	يُنْفِقُونْ	شَيْءْ
شُهَدَاءَ	زَوْجَيْنِ	ضَلَلٍ	أَلْبَابِ
شُهَدَاءْ	زَوْجَيْنْ	ضَلَلْ	أَلْبَابْ
مُصَلًّى	ضُحَى	رَقِيبًا	الْعُلَمَاءُ
مُصَلًّا	ضُحَا	رَقِيبَا	الْعُلَمَاءْ
تَنَمَّرَهُ	كُوِّرَتْ	ثَمَنِيَّةٌ	أَبِي
تَنَمَّرَهْ	كُوِّرَتْ	ثَمَنِيَّةْ	أَبْ

حروف مقطعات کا تلفظ

SHORT FORMS OF VERSES (LETTERS)

LESSON : 134

درس : ۱۳۴

بچے کو ان حروف کا تلفظ اچھی طرح سمجھا دیا جائے۔

The child should be taught the pronunciation of these words carefully.

طٰہٰ   الٓمٓصٓ   الٓمٓرٰ   الٓرٰ   الٓمٓ

طٰہٰ   الف لام میم صاد   الف لام میم را   الف لام را   الف لام میم

کٓهٰیٰعٓصٓ   عٓسٓقٓ   طٰسٓمٓ   طٰسٓ   یٰسٓ

کاف ہا یا عین صاد   عین سین قاف   طا سین میم   طا سین   یا سین

حٰمٓ   نٓ   قٓ   صٓ

حامیم   نون   قاف   صاد

سجدات و سورتوں کی تعداد

سجدۂ تلاوت قرآن شریف میں چودہ ہیں اور فوراً ادا کریں یا بعد میں۔ سجدے والی آیت جب پڑھی جائے تو پڑھنے والے اور سننے والے دونوں پر سجدہ کرنا لازم ہو جاتا ہے۔

تمام قرآن مجید میں کل ایک سو چودہ سورتیں ہیں۔ الحمد شریف کا نام سورت فاتحہ ہے۔

Prostrations (during reading the Holy Qur'an) are fourteen in number, performed immediately or later on. When an Ayah with Sajda (prostration) is recited, prostration becomes compulsory on both the readers and the listeners. There are One Hundred and Fourteen Chapters in the Holy Qur'an in all. The name of the opening Chapter (Al-Hamd Shareef) is Surat-al-Fatiha.

قرآن شریف کو بے وضو کو کبھی ہاتھ نہیں لگانا چاہیئے۔ ہاں بے وضو پڑھنا جائز ہے۔ باوضو پڑھنے میں زیادہ ثواب ہے۔

INSTRUCTION: The Holy Qur'an should never be touched without Wudu'. It is al-right to read it without Wudu'. There is more reward with Allah in reading the Holy Qur'an with Wudu'.